INFOGRAPHIC
HUMAN BODY

Kevin Pettman

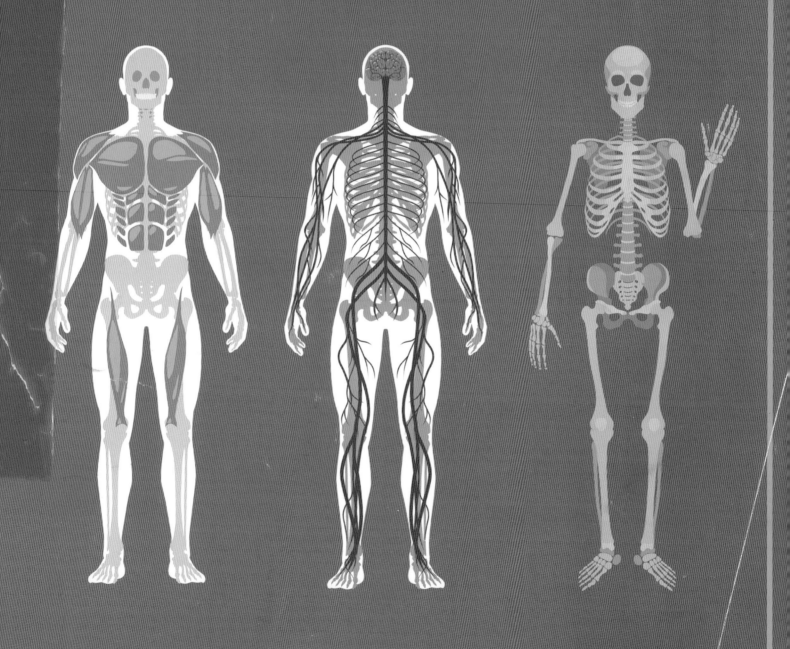

ARCTURUS

This edition published in 2020 by Arcturus Publishing Limited
26/27 Bickels Yard, 151–153 Bermondsey Street,
London SE1 3HA

Author: Kevin Pettman
Illustrator: Martin Sanders
Editor: Violet Peto
Designer: Nathan Balsom
Science Consultant: Kristina Routh
Art Direction: Rosie Bellwood
Managing Editor: Joe Harris

ISBN: 978-1-83857-518-2
CH007351NT
Supplier 29, Date 0420, Print run 9291

Printed in China

CONTENTS

WELCOME TO THE HUMAN BODY

The human body
is the most
amazing machine.
It is made up of **206 bones**, **79 organs**,
lots of **water**, trillions of **cells**, and
millions more clever things such as
nerves, **ligaments**, **muscles**, and **hairs**.
No human-made creation
can compare to the body—
each person is special and
unique, just like you!

The **best scientific** and **medical experts** in history have studied what makes the **body so brilliant**. From breathing and **eating** to **moving, growing, thinking**, and **fighting disease**, your body is constantly performing extraordinary feats. This **infographic human body guide** reveals all of the secrets behind them. It has **everything you need to know** about **how**, and **why**, the body does its **life-saving work**.

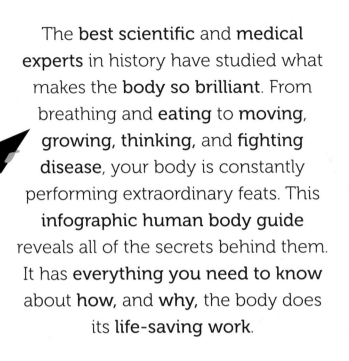

The **facts and figures** about the body may seem **brain-busting** and **frighten you to the bone!** Do not worry, because this book **explains everything** in a clear and fun way. It uses **simple, striking pictures, smart graphics**, and **direct, to-the-point language** to help you **grasp the information**. Each chapter looks at a part or system of the body, or job that it does. **You will build up your understanding** of what happens both on the **inside** and the **outside** and **learn weird** and **wonderful details**.

It is time to start your journey around the human body. Take a deep breath, turn the page, and let your eyes explore!

BUILDING BLOCKS

Some of the body's most important parts can be seen from the outside — such as eyes, ears, legs, arms, feet, hands, and teeth. Inside the body, there is a lot going on, too — the bones, organs, tissues, and cells are all hard at work in there!

This chapter looks at the **building blocks of the body** on the outside and inside.

How do cells work?

What are our most important organs, and what jobs do things like skin, hair, and nails do?

What elements and chemicals are we made of?

There are **lots of facts and numbers** to explore. Start building up your knowledge right away!

ESSENTIAL ELEMENTS

The human body is packed with lots of chemical elements that are essential for life. From metals to water, these substances all play key roles in keeping your body working properly.

BODY BREAKDOWN

Just **six elements** make up **99%** of the body's **weight**.

Oxygen
65%

Carbon
18.5%

Hydrogen
9.5%

Nitrogen
3.2%

Phosphorus
1%

Calcium
1.5%

Five of the other elements essential for human life are found in much smaller amounts.

Potassium
0.4%

Sulfur
0.3%

Sodium
0.2%

Chlorine
0.2%

Magnesium
0.2%

Iron

helps to carry oxygen in the blood.

Many more **elements** are found in tiny (trace) amounts, including iron (Fe), iodine (I), copper (Cu), silicon (Si), and zinc (Zn).

Zinc

helps the **immune system**, which protects the body against infections and germs.

Fe

I

Cu

Si

Zn

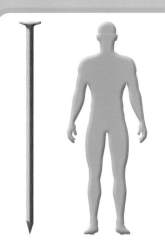

The body has **tiny amounts of metals** that are also found in everyday objects. one person has the same **amount of iron** as a 7.6 cm (3 inch) nail.

Diamonds are made from **carbon,** the same element that makes up 18.5% of a person's body weight. The average adult has the **same amount of carbon** in their body as **57,000 10-carat diamonds.**

Oxygen and hydrogen
are also found in the form of water inside the body.

Humans are made up of between **50%** and **70%** water!

70% Water

In a country with a mild climate, the body needs about **1.2 l (41 fl oz)** of water a day to work normally. **That's 6–8 glasses.** Living in a hotter country, or doing a lot of exercise, means the body needs more water.

When athletes work hard, they can lose **6–10% of their body weight through sweating.** Drinking water replaces this lost liquid.

CLOSE UP ON CELLS

Every living thing is made up of cells—they are the basis for life for humans, plants, and animals. These incredible, microscopic structures are in every part of the body, from the brain to your little toe!

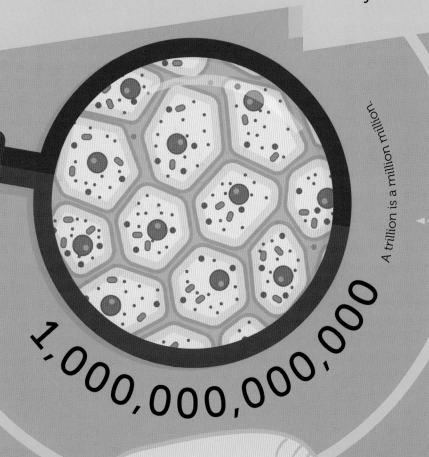

A trillion is a million million.

1,000,000,000,000

There are between
30 and 40 trillion cells
in the body.

The body grows from a single cell.

This splits **again** and **again** to keep making more cells. Cells keep growing and dying all the time—about
300 million die every minute!

Even the tip of your little finger has **billions of cells** inside it.

LOOK INSIDE A HUMAN CELL

Membrane
This acts like a wall to protect the cell, a little like skin. It lets some substances in and stops others.

Mitochondria
These make energy. Nutrients from digested food react with oxygen to give the body energy.

Cytoplasm
This is mostly water and is where the parts of the cell float around and many chemical reactions happen.

Lysosome
This is a tiny bag that holds enzymes for digesting worn-out cell parts

Ribosomes
These make proteins. Proteins do lots of things, including helping the body move and be strong.

Nucleus
The nucleus controls the cell and tells it what to do.

The structures inside a cell, such as the mitochondria and ribosomes, are called **organelles**.

There are over **200** different types of human cells.

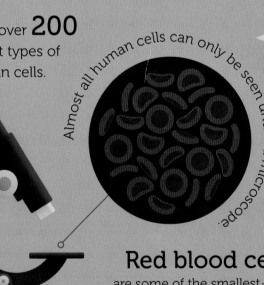

Almost all human cells can only be seen under a microscope.

Red blood cells
are some of the smallest—125 of them in a row are only **1 mm (0.04 in) long!** That's about the same width as this dot.

A human egg cell is about **10 times bigger** than a red blood cell.

The **giant egg** of an ostrich is the largest-known cell.

DISCOVER DNA AND GENES

Two of the most fascinating building blocks of the body are DNA and the genes they carry. Invisible to the human eye, they play a big part in how we grow, how we behave, and what we look like.

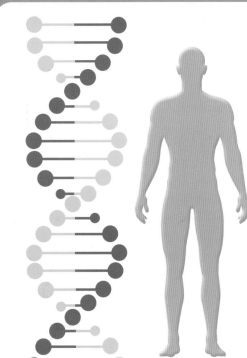

Inside the nucleus of cells is **deoxyribonucleic** acid, known as DNA.

It is a chemical with **two long spiral molecules.** This is called a **double-helix structure.**

There are about **3 billion pairs** of DNA building blocks in each cell.

Stretched out, all the **DNA** from one cell would be about **2 m (6 ft 5 in) long.** That's much longer than the height of an average adult male.

If all the **DNA** in all your cells was stretched out, it would be able to span about the **diameter of our solar system twice!**

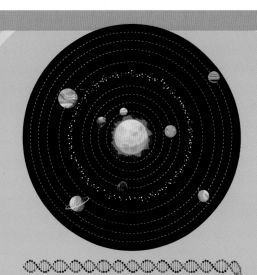

DNA
is a bit like **computer coding.** A cell gets instructions from the code and knows what to do inside the body.

Each DNA string carries instructions called **genes.**

Genes help cells make proteins.
They control things like the **weight** and **height** you are likely to be as an adult and what your **eyes**, **ears**, and **nose** look like.

Genes are inherited (passed on) to a person from their **mother and father.**

DNA DUTIES

The job of DNA is to tell cells what to do. Cells are responsible for the **growth and survival** of every structure in the body, like the brain, lungs, heart, and blood.

Parents pass on **23 chromosomes** each when a baby is created. A mother always passes on an **X chromosome,** but a father provides an **X or Y chromosome.**

Two **X chromosomes** means that a baby will be a girl, and an **X and Y chromosome** means it will be a boy.

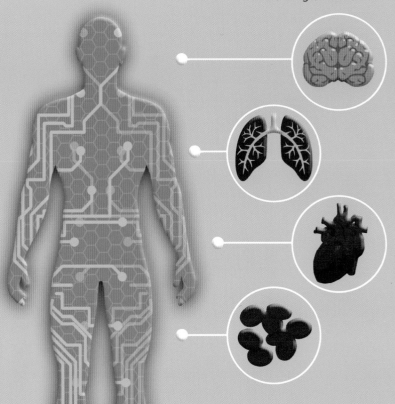

A **chromosome** is a collection of lots of genes and is made up of **DNA.**

Humans have **46 chromosomes** in each cell. This number is different in other living things ...

About 99.9% of DNA is exactly the same for every human on Earth.

99.9%

The 0.1% is what makes every person different!

A red king crab has **208** chromosomes.

A dog has **78** chromosomes.

A fruit fly has **8** chromosomes.

ORGANS AND SYSTEMS

There are nearly 80 organs inside the body. Groups of organs work together in systems to carry out vital tasks such as breathing, digesting food, getting rid of waste, and sending messages.

ORGAN DUTIES

A group of **cells** working together to do the same job forms **tissue**. A collection of tissues that helps the body do something is an **organ**.

There are **five organs** that are very important for the body to survive:

1. Brain
This is the body's HQ. It controls all organs by sending and receiving messages.

2. Lungs
These take in oxygen for the blood and remove carbon dioxide.

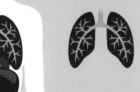

3. Liver
Among other things, the liver cleans the blood and stores energy.

4. Heart
This powerful pump squeezes blood around the body.

5. Kidneys
These remove waste and fluid from the blood.

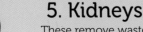

In total, the body has
79 organs.

The liver is the
largest organ
inside the body.

An adult's liver weighs an average of **1.4 kg (3 lb)**, which is about the weight of
12 muffins.

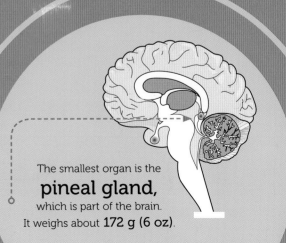

The smallest organ is the
pineal gland,
which is part of the brain.
It weighs about **172 g (6 oz)**.

SPECIAL SYSTEM

Certain organs cooperate in groups known as organ systems.

The body has 11 organ systems including:

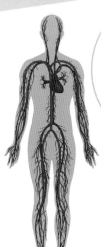

Nervous system
This is the body's messenger system, made up of the brain, spinal cord, and a network of nerves.

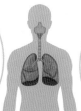

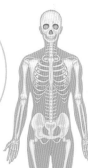

Digestive system
Food is broken down and passed through the body via the digestive system.

Muscular system
This system uses muscles to help the body move.

Circulatory system
Our circulatory system is responsible for moving blood, oxygen, and carbon dioxide around the body.

Respiratory system
This system enables the body to breathe.

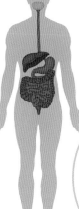

Skeletal system
Made up of bones, tendons, ligaments, and cartilage, the skeletal system gives the body strength and movement.

Other important **organ systems** are:

Integumentary system
This system protects the body from the outside. It includes skin, hair, and nails.

Lymphatic system
This keeps fluid balanced within the body and carries white blood cells to fight infections.

Urinary system
The urinary system removes waste liquid from the body.

Endocrine system
The endocrine system puts hormones into the blood to regulate bodily functions.

Reproductive system
This system enables the body to make a baby.

Some scientists say that the immune system, which protects us from germs, is an **organ system by itself.**

Other experts argue that the immune system is part of the **lymphatic system.**

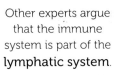

Blood has the vital job of taking **oxygen from the lungs to cells in the body,** but it is not called an organ.

It is a **connective tissue and a fluid,** which means blood has no fixed shape.

SKETCH OUT THE SKELETON

Without a skeleton, your body could not move. It would be a blob on the ground! Human bones are strong but light and help the body in unexpected ways.

MADE FOR THIS

The skeleton is made up of all the bones inside the human body.

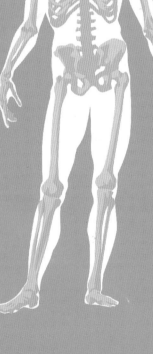

The skeleton has four main jobs:

1. To support the body and keep it upright.

2. To help the body move.

3. To protect organs such as the heart and lungs.

4. To make blood cells, which transport oxygen and nutrients, and fight germs.

The skeleton makes up about **15%** of an adult's total body weight.

15%

An insect's skeleton is on the outside, and is called an exoskeleton.

Humans and other vertebrates have a **skeleton on the inside.** This is called an **endoskeleton.**

The skeleton is **super strong.** A piece of bone is **four times stronger** than a piece of concrete that is the same weight.

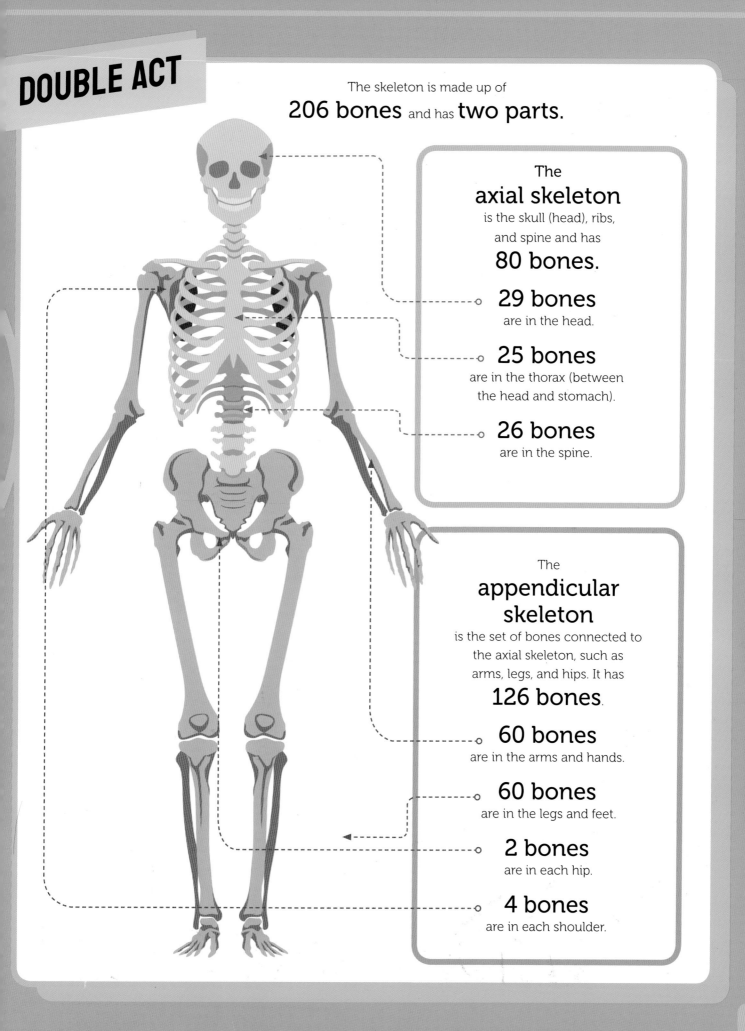

DOUBLE ACT

The skeleton is made up of
206 bones and has **two parts.**

The
axial skeleton
is the skull (head), ribs,
and spine and has
80 bones.

29 bones
are in the head.

25 bones
are in the thorax (between
the head and stomach).

26 bones
are in the spine.

The
appendicular skeleton
is the set of bones connected to
the axial skeleton, such as
arms, legs, and hips. It has
126 bones.

60 bones
are in the arms and hands.

60 bones
are in the legs and feet.

2 bones
are in each hip.

4 bones
are in each shoulder.

CLOSE TO THE BONE

With over 200 bones inside a human, there are many different types, shapes, and sizes to discover. Take a tour of the body to learn more about these awesome support structures!

Bones come in
5 basic types:

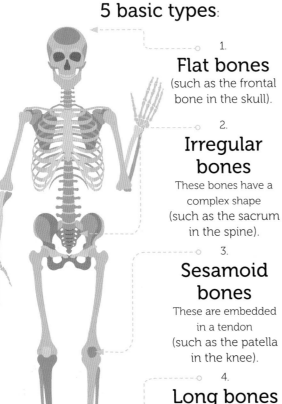

1.
Flat bones
(such as the frontal bone in the skull).

2.
Irregular bones
These bones have a complex shape (such as the sacrum in the spine).

3.
Sesamoid bones
These are embedded in a tendon (such as the patella in the knee).

4.
Long bones
(such as the femur in the leg).

5.
Short bones
(such as the tarsal bone in the foot).

Bones contain a mineral called calcium phosphate. A person's bones have
99%
of all the body's calcium.

INSIDE KNOWLEDGE

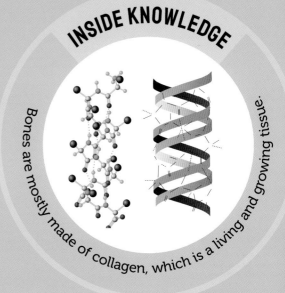

Bones are mostly made of collagen, which is a living and growing tissue.

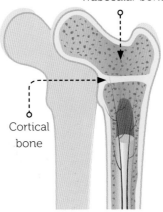

Trabecular bone

Cortical bone

Outer bone   Inner bone

Bones have two layers.
Cortical bone
is the strong outer layer, and
trabecular bone
is the softer, spongy inner layer.

Cortical bone makes up
80%
of the total weight of the body's bones.

Bones are light inside and are a little bit like the
honeycomb
inside a bee's nest.
If bones were **solid and heavy**, it would be difficult for the body to move!

More than
50%
of the body's 206 bones are found in the **hands and feet!**

20

A baby has about
300 bones,
which is around 100 more than
an adult. As a child grows, many
of its bones **fuse together to
form fewer, bigger bones,**
until it only has 206.

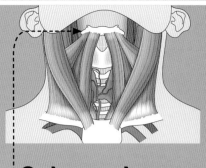

°**Only one bone**
is not connected to any other bone
in the body. This is the hyoid.

The
hyoid bone
is in the neck and helps
the tongue move.

The
oldest human bones
ever discovered are between
**300,000 to 350,000
years old.**

The bones, known
as **remains
or fossils**,
were found in
Africa in 2017.

They came from
five people
who were
**a type of
early human.**

Bones grow becoming larger and heavier until a human is about 20 years old.

GET UNDER THE SKIN

Both inside and outside, the skin is a very special organ. It keeps harmful things away, helps you stay warm or cool, and protects against sunlight.

SIZE AND WEIGHT

Skin is the largest organ in the body.
In adults, it can weigh around 4 kg (9 lb), which is about the weight of **four pineapples**.

Skin is thin but tough.
Eyelid skin is the thinnest,
at approximately
0.5 mm (0.02 in).

Males usually have thicker skin than females.

The thickest skin is between **4** and **5 mm** (0.16 and 0.2 in). It's found on the soles of the **feet** and palms of the **hands**.

Skin bends and stretches
with every move you make.

Stretched out, the average adult skin would cover an area of around
2 m² (22 sq ft).
That's larger than an ice hockey goal!

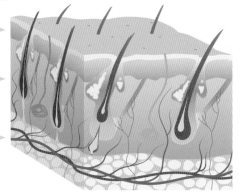

LAYER LESSON

Epidermis

Dermis

Hypodermis

The **epidermis** is the outer skin layer. Its main jobs are to protect the body from germs and to make it waterproof.

The inner **dermis** layer has sweat and oil glands. It also has blood vessels and nerve endings, which send messages to the brain when our senses detect things like touch, pain, and temperature.

The layer beneath the dermis is the **hypodermis**. It stores body fat and absorbs shocks that hit the skin.

If skin didn't
keep water out,

the body would swell
up in the bath!

People with
light skin
have melanin in the skin's lower
layers only and
need more
sunscreen
to protect them.

People with
dark skin
have more melanin in all layers.

BRIGHT IDEA

A brown chemical called melanin is made by the skin and helps to safely soak up some of this light. The skin gives some protection against harmful ultraviolet sunlight.

The skin has
millions of bacteria.
Bacteria are microscopic living
organisms.

Skin folds, such
as the armpit, are warmer
and more moist and let more
bacteria grow.

Skin is constantly dying and being
rubbed off from the body, with
25,000 bacteria shed
every minute.
New skin, from the
dermis layer, replaces it.

Skin repairs
itself after a cut,
burn, or injury.
The body makes a blood clot
in the wound, with the top layer
drying to create a scab.

THE HAIR-RAISING TRUTH

There are hundreds of thousands of hairs all over the body. Discover why and how hairs grow, what hair does, and why having a haircut is not painful!

The hair on a head is often the **thickest and longest.** Each hair grows for between 2 and 7 years on average.

Long hair helps protect a human's scalp, which is the skin covering the top of the head. It shields the head from sunlight, and also keeps it warm in cold weather.

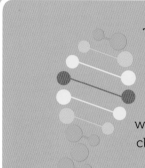

The length of time hair grows for **depends on genes,** which are instructions for characteristics passed on by our parents.

If one or both of a **person's parents can grow long hair,** it's likely that person will, too, as they will have that **same gene.**

COUNTDOWN

Hair grows all over the skin but not on the lips, soles of the feet, or palms of the hands. These skin parts **do not have hair follicles.**

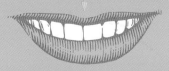

The average person has about **100,000 hairs** on their head. This number changes depending on the shade of the hair.

Red averages 90,000 hairs.

Brown averages 110,000 hairs.

Black averages 100,000 hairs.

Fair averages 150,000 hairs.

Hair is the body's second fastest growing tissue, at around 1 cm (0.4 in) growth a month. Only bone marrow, the spongy substance in bones, grows faster.

Humans have around **420** eyelashes, **600** eyebrow hairs, and **25,000** body hairs.

GROW UP

Follicles are tiny pockets in the skin

where hair grows. Each hair grows from a **root in the follicle**, which is fed from the body's blood.

As hair pushes up through the skin, a gland next to it releases oil.

This makes the hair shiny and waterproof.

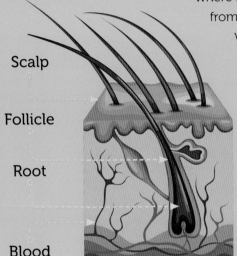

Scalp

Follicle

Root

Blood vessel

Hair had died

by the time it pokes through the skin.

This is why having a haircut doesn't hurt!

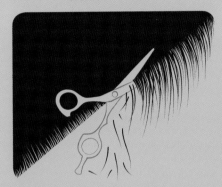

Humans are born with all their hair follicles, which is about

5 million.

STAGE SHOW

Head hair has three stages of life.

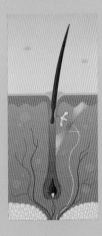

1. **The growth stage,** also known as the anagen stage. This can last 2–7 years.

2. **The catagen stage** usually lasts for 2–3 weeks and is the end of hair growth.

3. **The telogen stage** is when hair rests and begins to fall out and be replaced by new hair again.

It's natural for a person to lose hair from their head.

We can lose between 50 and 100 hairs a day!

TOUGH AS NAILS

Every one of our fingers and toes has a nail on the end. Those 20 nails all need to be looked after to stay healthy as the body grows older and changes.

NAILED IT

Nails begin in the nail root, under the nail cuticle.

Cells in the root **grow and push,** sliding along the nail bed.

Nail plate

Nail tip

Nail plate

Nail bed

Lunula

Nail root

Cuticle

Nail matrix

Nails are flattened and hardened because they are made from a **tough material called keratin.**

When a nail pokes out of the skin, **the cells inside it have died.** That's why it doesn't hurt to have nails cut.

COOL CUTICLE

A cuticle protects the new nail and surrounding skin from infection.

The cuticle is the tiny layer of clear skin on the bottom edge of the nail.

Nails protect the ends of fingers and toes.

Fingernails also help humans pick up objects by letting the fingertips press against them.

SLOW PROGRESS

Fingernails and toenails
grow very slowly.
On average, fingernails grow
about 3 mm (0.12 in) a month.

Toenails grow even slower
—about just **1 mm (0.04 in)** every month. Some scientists think this is because less blood reaches the feet, which slows growth.

The longer the bones in the finger,
the longer the nail grows. A person's middle finger usually has the longest and quickest-growing nail.

If a fingernail falls off because of injury, it will grow back in around
6 months.

It's thought that nails grow
quicker in summer
because the warmer weather increases blood flow to the fingers.

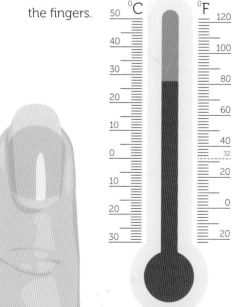

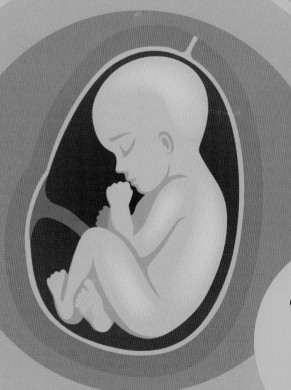

A baby's nails grow even before it is born.
When a mother has been pregnant for around
11 weeks,
her baby's nails begin to take shape.

KNOW THE NERVOUS SYSTEM

Your **nervous system** is amazing! It's more powerful than any computer on the planet. And just like a computer, it can deal with **billions** of messages and instructions in just a fraction of a second!

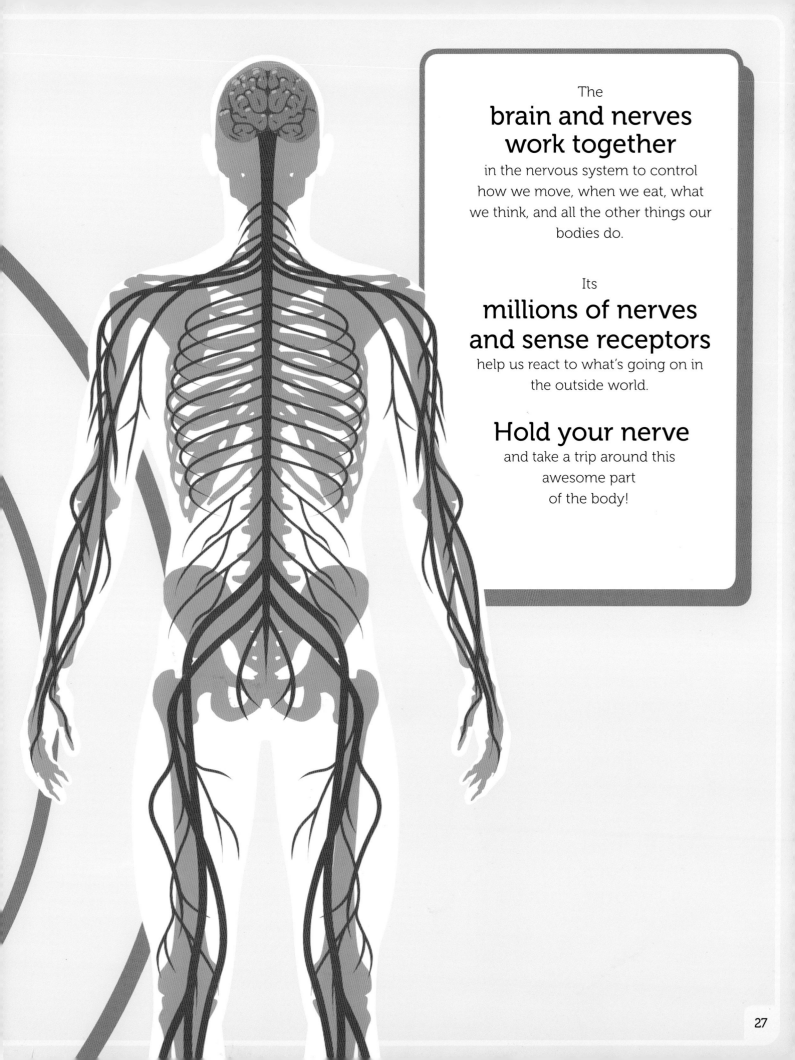

The
brain and nerves work together
in the nervous system to control how we move, when we eat, what we think, and all the other things our bodies do.

Its
millions of nerves and sense receptors
help us react to what's going on in the outside world.

Hold your nerve
and take a trip around this awesome part of the body!

THE BRILLIANT BRAIN

It's time to get ahead! Take a look inside the brain and discover lots of fascinating facts about how this amazing organ works, and what it does.

The brain has three main sections—the **cerebral cortex, the cerebellum,** and the **brainstem.**

The cerebral cortex is the outer layer. It is folded into deep wrinkles, and it has four parts that do different things:

1. The
frontal lobe
controls thinking, moving, making decisions, and reasoning.

2. The
parietal lobe
makes sense of messages about taste, touch, and temperature.

3. The
occipital lobe
takes information from the eyes.

4. The
temporal lobe
looks after sound, speech, and memory.

The **cerebellum** helps with movement and balance.

The **brainstem** is at the bottom and is connected to the spinal cord. It controls things you don't think about, such as breathing, heartbeat, and the kidneys.

The brain is like a
computer controlling everything
a person does.

It can get about
11 million messages a second
from the rest of the body!

The average adult brain weighs 1.3 kg (2.9 lb). That's the weight of a small toaster.

About **75%** **of the brain** **is water.**
If the body is dehydrated (has less water than it needs), this affects how the brain works.

Wearing a helmet protects the skull and brain during activities like cycling and horse-riding.

The **22 skull bones** in the head protect the brain from injury.

It makes up **2%** of a human's total weight, but it uses **20%** of the body's energy.

The brain has about **100 billion neurons.**
A neuron is a nerve cell and it acts like a **tiny wire carrying a signal.**

R   L

R   L

Scientists think the **left part of the brain controls the right side of the body** and the **right part of the brain looks after the body's left side.**

Each neuron makes a very small amount of electricity, but together they could **power a light bulb.**

SEND A MESSAGE

All the millions of nerve signals speeding around the body rely on the nervous system. The brain and nerves must act together for all the commands, alerts, and other pieces of information to be understood.

The nervous system controls all our movements and thoughts.

It has two parts:
the central nervous system and the **peripheral nervous system.**

The central nervous system (CNS) is the brain and the spinal cord.
The peripheral nervous system is all the other nerves in the rest of the body.

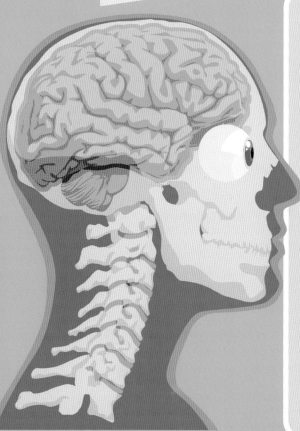

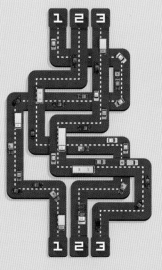

There are
billions
of long threadlike structures connecting neurons in the brain. They act like a network of roads, carrying information and messages to and from the brain.

Messages can move between neurons at a speed of over
400 km/h
(250 mph).
That's faster than a racing car!

When neurons connect, they make
a pathway.
These pathways help the brain remember things it has learned.

There are **two main types** of nerves:

... let the brain control muscles, so that the body can move. Signals travel down **motor nerves** in only one direction —**away from the brain.**

Sensory nerves ...

... take signals from the **five senses** of touch, sight, taste, smell, and hearing. Sensory nerve signals travel one way —**to the brain.**

 Nerves work by two powerful processes. These are **chemical and electrical actions.**

The **spinal cord** runs from the bottom of the brain, through the neck, and down toward the bottom of the back.

In adults, the spinal cord's average length is **45 cm (18 in) for men and 43 cm (17 in) for women.**

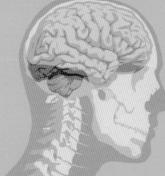

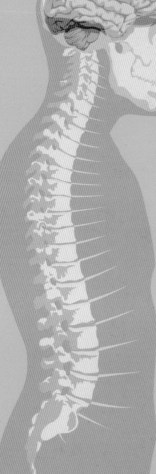

The spinal cord has **31 sections.**

Each section of the spinal cord has one pair of nerves leaving it. **That's 62 nerves in total.**

There are **12 pairs of nerves** that come direct from the brain and not via the spinal cord. These are **cranial nerves.**

 When receptors in parts of the body such as the hands and feet feel things like **heat and pain,** urgent messages are sent via nerves to the **central nervous system.**

SPEAKING OUT

Humans are almost certainly the only animals that talk to each other using complex language. The brain controls and makes sense of everything we say and hear when we're speaking together.

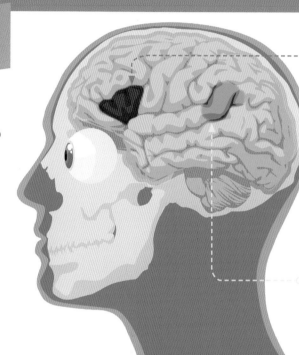

The brain has two important areas
that help us understand and use words and language.

Broca's and **Wernicke's** areas are both in the left side of the brain.

Broca's area
helps a person to produce speech.

Wernicke's area
interprets the words a person hears and reads.

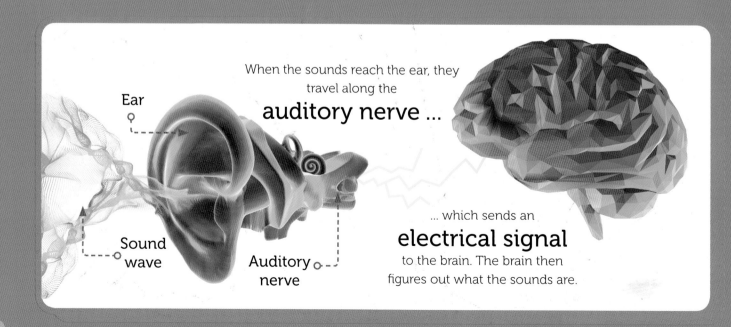

When the sounds reach the ear, they travel along the
auditory nerve ...

Ear

Sound wave

Auditory nerve

... which sends an
electrical signal
to the brain. The brain then figures out what the sounds are.

A baby usually makes babbling and gurgling sounds at around **five months old.**

Goo-goo, gaa-gaa.

At about **one year old,** babies begin to make sounds from the language they hear spoken around them.

The brain **controls the movement of the lips and tongue** to help us to speak.

Different positions
of the lips

make certain sounds.

CIAO!

It seems to be easier for a person to **learn a second language** under the age of about **13 years old.**

BONJOUR, HOLA, GUTEN TAG, CIAO, OLA, NAMASTE, SALAAM, KONNICHIWA

After this age, it **becomes more difficult** because as we get older, more of the brain is needed to understand another language.

People who can speak two languages are called **bilingual.**

The tongue moves against the top of the mouth or the teeth to make other sounds.

FEELING EMOTIONAL

People feel a wide range of emotions, such as happiness, sadness, or surprise, at different times. Emotions are processed and controlled in the brain.

Feelings and emotions are made in the brain, in the part of the brain called the **limbic system.**

The limbic system has

four main sections

that create our emotions and feelings—the **hippocampus, amygdala, hypothalamus,** and **thalamus** sections.

A human brain has two of each of these sections, with one in each half of the brain.

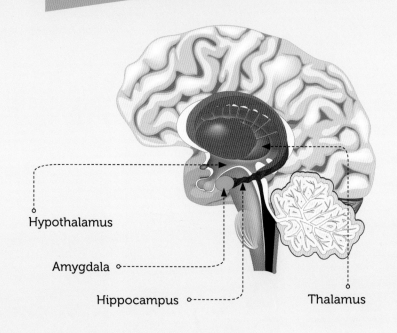

Hypothalamus

Amygdala

Hippocampus

Thalamus

FACE FACTS

The expression on a face often reveals if a person is feeling any of the **six basic emotions:**

Happiness
A big, friendly smile.

Sadness
Pupils (the black spots in the middle of the eyes) are smaller, and lips puff out and drop down.

Fear
Open mouth with raised eyebrows and upper lip.

Anger
Lowered eyebrows and teeth clenched together.

Disgust
Wide lips, narrowed eyes, and screwed-up nose.

Surprise
Raised eyebrows, wrinkles on the forehead, and wide eyes.

Sometimes we feel a mixture of emotions. For example, crying can be as a result of sadness and fear.

When we feel emotions, the brain may send nerve signals to other parts of the body, making us react.

For example, **anger** could cause the heart **to beat faster.**

Fear may make a person **run away** from danger.

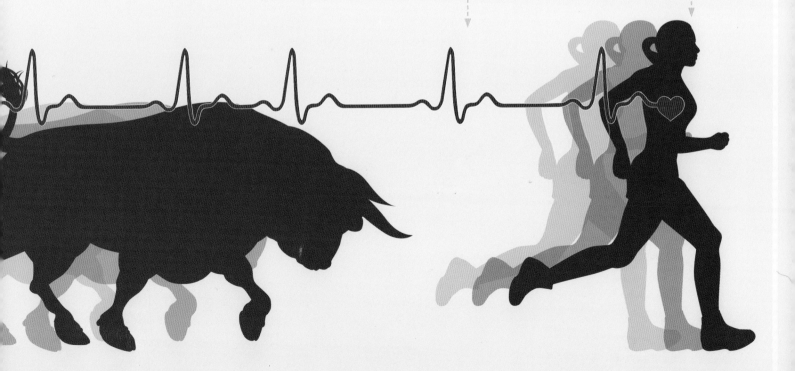

WHAT'S THAT SMELL?

The human nose is very sensitive and can smell all kinds of things. It sends messages about the smells it detects along nerves to the brain, so the brain can figure out what they are.

KNOW THE NOSE

The two holes in your nose are nostrils

When you breathe in, **chemicals in the air enter your nose through the nostrils**.

The space inside the head behind the nose is the **nasal cavity.**

Brain

Olfactory bulb

Nasal cavity

Above the top of the nasal cavity is the **olfactory bulb.**

The **olfactory bulb sends signals** about the chemical smells in the cavity along nerves to the brain.

Special hairs containing **receptors** lie at the back of the nasal cavity.

The hairs cover an area about the size of a **postage stamp.**

A human nose has about **350 types of olfactory receptors.**

Rats have a much stronger sense of smell than humans—with about **1,400 types of olfactory receptors!**

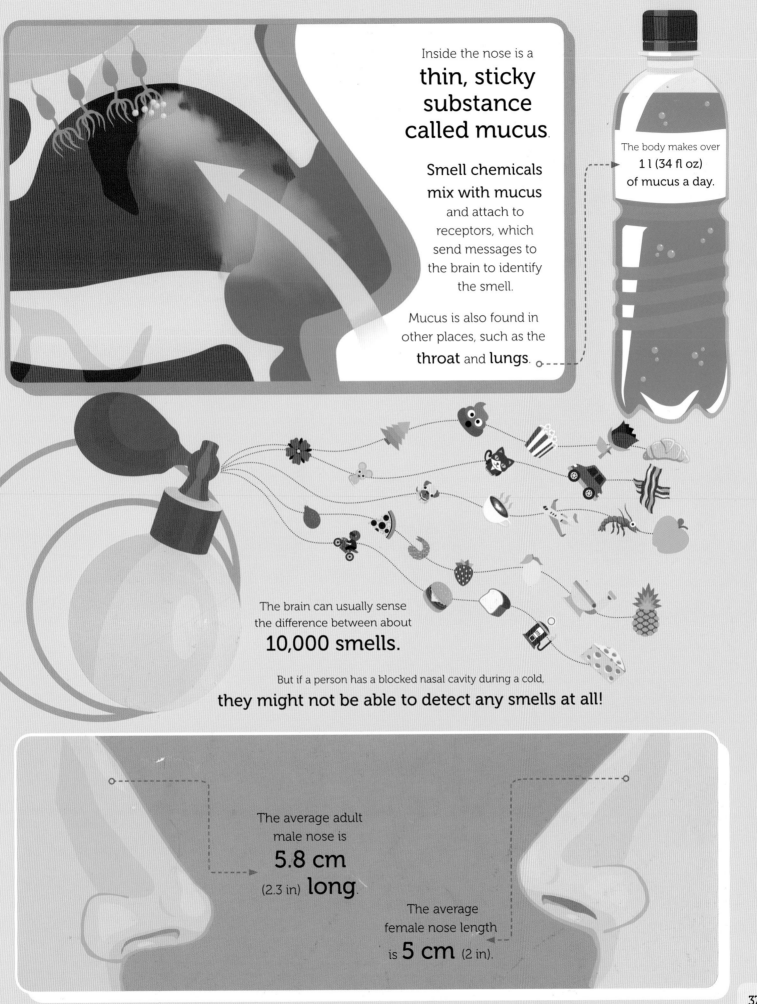

Inside the nose is a

thin, sticky substance called mucus.

Smell chemicals mix with mucus and attach to receptors, which send messages to the brain to identify the smell.

Mucus is also found in other places, such as the **throat** and **lungs.**

The body makes over **1 l (34 fl oz)** of mucus a day.

The brain can usually sense the difference between about

10,000 smells.

But if a person has a blocked nasal cavity during a cold,

they might not be able to detect any smells at all!

The average adult male nose is

5.8 cm
(2.3 in) **long.**

The average female nose length is **5 cm** (2 in).

TASTY TREAT

The sense of taste helps your body to figure out what it likes to eat and drink. The tongue and its nerves play the starring roll in this mouthwatering mission!

Nerves in the tongue send signals to the brain, and the brain combines them with smell signals to work out what food and drink tastes like.

Your tongue contains around **10,000** taste buds!

The pink and white bumps all over the top of the tongue are papillae.

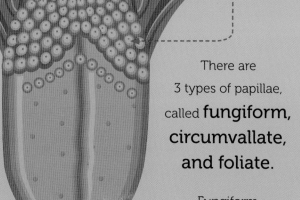

There are 3 types of papillae, called **fungiform, circumvallate, and foliate.**

Fungiform **are too small to see** with the human eye, but the other two can be seen.

Each papillae on the tongue can contain **hundreds of taste buds.**

Each **taste bud** helps the brain to detect the different tastes in food.

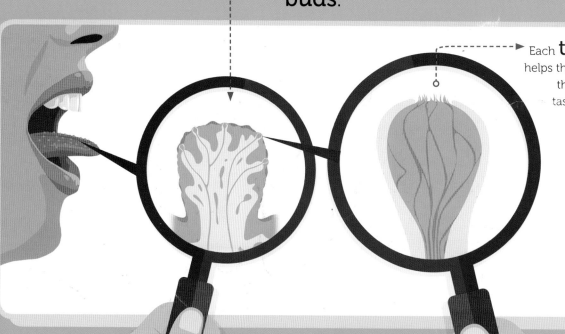

Taste buds are usually replaced every two weeks or so. But as we get older some are not replaced. By the age of 65, a person may have just

5,000 buds,

which means they can sense fewer tastes.

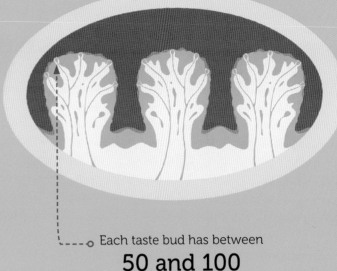

Each taste bud has between

50 and 100
sense receptors.

These send signals along the nerves to the brain.

TOP TASTIES

The tongue can pick out five main tastes:

1. Sweet

2. Sour

3. Salty

4. Umami

5. Bitter

Some taste buds can detect only

one of the five

types of taste, while others can detect all of them.

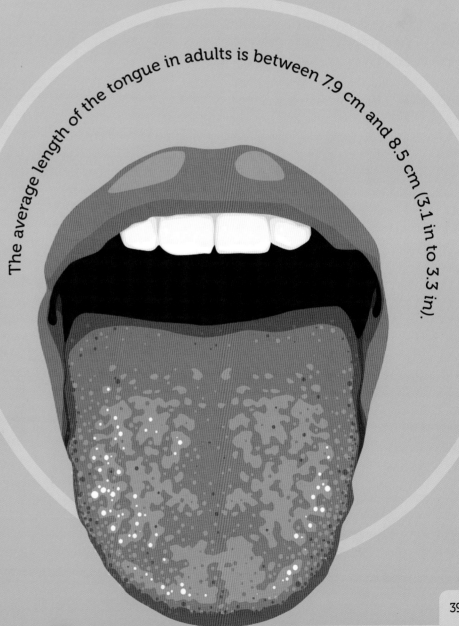

The average length of the tongue in adults is between 7.9 cm and 8.5 cm (3.1 in to 3.3 in).

GET IN TOUCH

The nervous system has special ways to help the body sense different things through touch. For example, we can sense hot, cold, and painful things very quickly and easily.

SKIN DEEP

Touch is sensed by **millions of nerves** called **receptors** inside the skin.

Touch receptors send messages to the brain about different feelings of touch from all over the body.

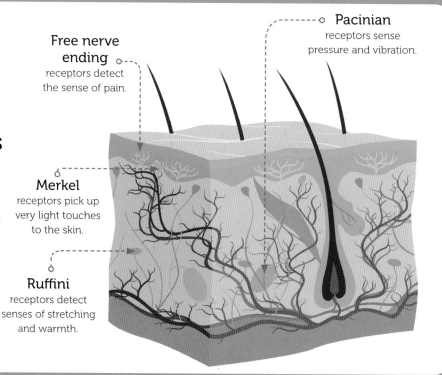

Free nerve ending receptors detect the sense of pain.

Pacinian receptors sense pressure and vibration.

Merkel receptors pick up very light touches to the skin.

Ruffini receptors detect senses of stretching and warmth.

HAPPY **18**th BIRTHDAY

The body **loses touch receptors** in the skin when it gets older. It's thought that we have the most touch receptors between the ages of **16** and **18**.

Skin is packed with heat receptors.

Dipping the elbow in a warm bath is a good way to sense how hot the water is.

The **nose and fingers** have lots of receptors that sense both heat and cold.

EASY TOUCH

Some parts of the body are **more sensitive to touch** than others, and have **lots of touch receptors** in them.

Four places that are very **sensitive** to touch:

Feet

Fingertips

Tongue

Lips

Four places that are **less sensitive** to touch:

Chest

Forearm

Calf (back of the leg)

Back

PINPOINT

A fingertip can sense **two separate pin touches** just **5 mm (0.2 in) apart.** This is because fingertips are very sensitive.

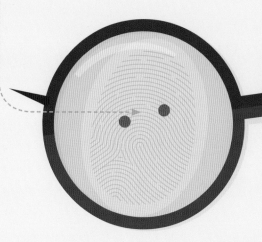

The skin of the forearm is less sensitive. **Two pin touches** that are around **40 mm (1.5 in) apart** may be detected as just one touch.

BRAILLE

Blind people interpret a written language called **Braille** by **feeling** a series of **raised dots** with their **fingertips.** Each pattern of dots makes a certain letter or number.

WHAT AN EYE-OPENER

Our eyes are small, but they play an important role. Their remarkable structure lets us see objects up close and far away. Come and take a peek at the pupil, iris, retina, lens, and other parts of these fascinating organs.

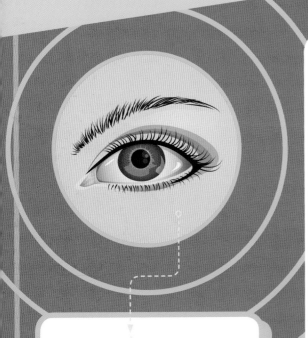

Eyes are very delicate and are protected by the bones of the socket, the eyelids, and eyelashes.

Each **eyeball sits in an eye socket** in the skull. The **eye is a little smaller than a table tennis ball,** with a diameter of about **2.4 cm** (0.9 in).

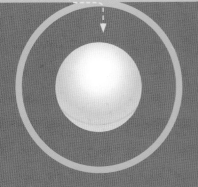

Each eye has **six muscles:**
lateral rectus, medial rectus, superior rectus, inferior rectus, superior oblique, and inferior oblique.

Superior oblique

Superior rectus

Medial rectus

Lateral rectus

Inferior rectus

Inferior oblique

Right eyeball

The muscles move the eye in different directions.

The two eye's muscles move together so **both eyes look at the same thing.**

The eyelids close and open automatically every **2–3 seconds.** Blinking helps the eyelids spread oil over the eye and keep the cornea moist.

The cornea is the clear surface at the front of the eye.

The black circle in the middle is called the **pupil.** The shaded area around the pupil is the **iris.**

When it's dark, muscles in the **iris** let the **pupil get bigger.** This lets in more light and makes things easier to see.

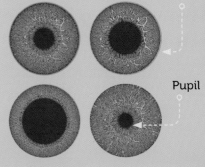

Iris

Pupil

The job of **eyelashes** is to keep harmful dust and dirt from getting into the eye.

When we sleep, our eyelids close. This blocks out light and keeps the **cornea from drying**.

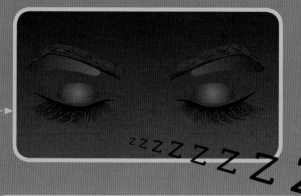

Light bends as it goes through the **cornea** and the **lens**. This turns the image on the **retina upside down**.

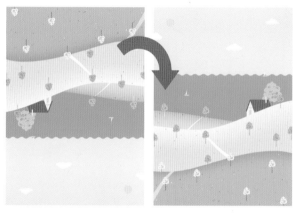

The brain receives a message from the retina, and flips the image the right way up.

Glasses can be worn to help light entering the eye focus properly on the retina.

Around 4 billion adults wear glasses.

The **lens is behind the pupil.**

When light enters the pupil, the lens helps focus it onto the **retina**.

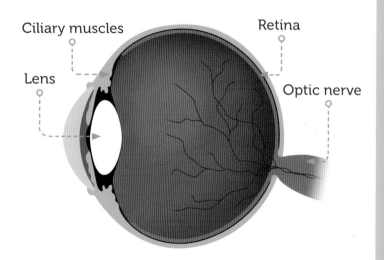

Ciliary muscles

Retina

Lens

Optic nerve

The **ciliary muscles** around the lens act to change the shape of the lens. This helps the lens **focus on things at different distances** from the eye.

The lens focuses an image in about
0.2 seconds.

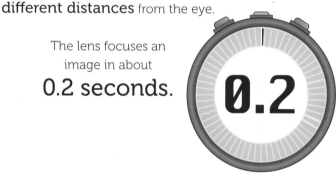

0.2

The **retina** is curved around the back of the eye. It has nerve cells called **rods and cones**.

There are about
130 million rods and 7 million cones.

The **optic nerve** carries messages from the rods and cones to the brain.

A part of the brain called the **visual cortex** deciphers the messages so the **brain "sees" images** from the eye.

LISTEN UP

Thanks to its clever network of canals, bones, nerves, and drum, the ear can pick up all kinds of sounds. Listen up for some epic info about the body's extraordinary listening powers.

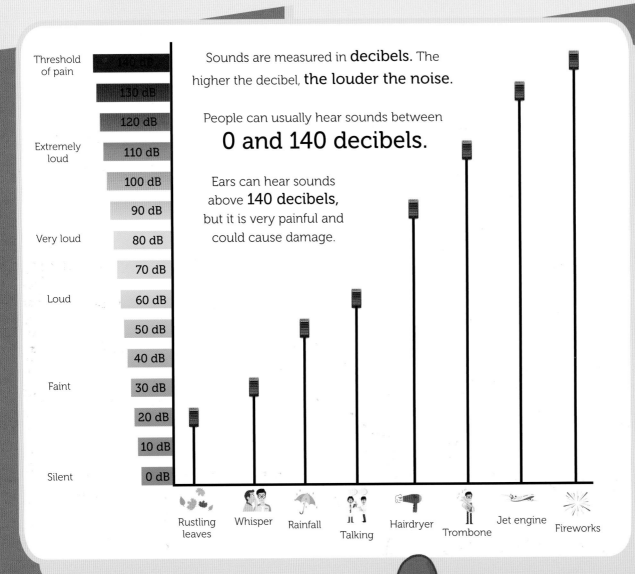

Sounds are measured in **decibels**. The higher the decibel, **the louder the noise.**

People can usually hear sounds between

0 and 140 decibels.

Ears can hear sounds above **140 decibels**, but it is very painful and could cause damage.

Threshold of pain	140 dB
	130 dB
	120 dB
Extremely loud	110 dB
	100 dB
	90 dB
Very loud	80 dB
	70 dB
Loud	60 dB
	50 dB
	40 dB
Faint	30 dB
	20 dB
	10 dB
Silent	0 dB

Rustling leaves · Whisper · Rainfall · Talking · Hairdryer · Trombone · Jet engine · Fireworks

The human ear has

three parts:

the outer ear, middle ear, and inner ear.

The outer ear is the part you can see. The medical term for the outer ear is the **pinna or auricle.**

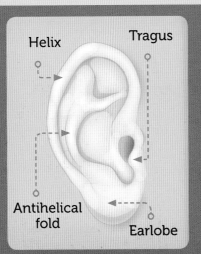

Helix · Tragus · Antihelical fold · Earlobe

The average adult outer ear is

6.3 cm (2.5 in) long.

That's about the size of the little finger.

The **ear canal** goes from the outer ear to the eardrum. The eardrum is between the outer and middle ear.

Sound waves

travel along the ear canal.

The eardrum is a thin piece of skin about

10 mm (0.4 in) wide.

The eardrum vibrates when sound reaches it. The vibrations rattle against **three small bones** called the **hammer, anvil,** and **stirrup.** Vibrations in these bones transfer the message to the inner ear.

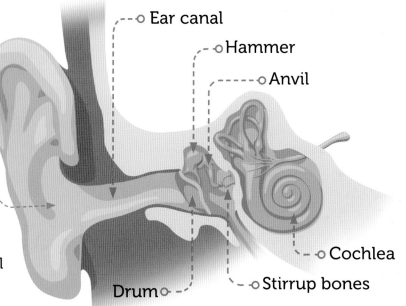

Ear canal
Hammer
Anvil
Cochlea
Stirrup bones
Drum

The cochlea is only about the size of a pea and looks like a snail's shell! In the inner ear is a rolled-up tube called the cochlea.

Vibrations from the inner ear are sent along the **auditory nerve** to the brain as electrical signals. The brain interprets these signals as sounds.

Earlobes come in **two** main shapes:

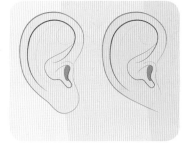

Free earlobes hang below the ear. **Attached earlobes** are connected to the side of the head and don't hang.

The outer ear sticks out because its job is to **collect sounds** from around the body.

Flaps and folds in the ear skin help to gather sounds. These include the **helix, tragus,** and **antihelical fold.**

ON THE MOVE

People can **move** in amazing ways. **Our legs** and **spine** carry us around, and our **eyes**, **ears**, and **brain** work together to help us move safely. There are lots of other important things going on inside the moving body, too. Our **bones**, **muscles**, **joints**, and **ligaments** are all part of the **incredible** human **moving machine**.

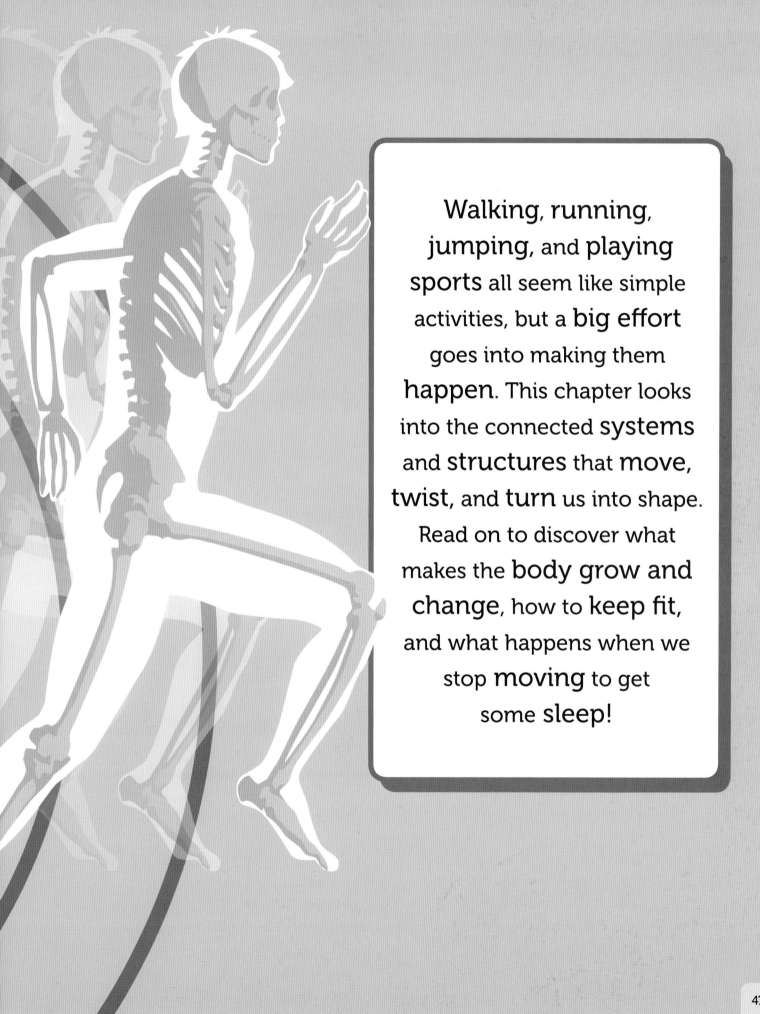

Walking, running, jumping, and playing sports all seem like simple activities, but a big effort goes into making them happen. This chapter looks into the connected systems and structures that move, twist, and turn us into shape. Read on to discover what makes the body grow and change, how to keep fit, and what happens when we stop moving to get some sleep!

FLEX YOUR MUSCLES

We can see our muscles hard at work under the skin in areas like the arm, leg, and back. But there are many more muscles hidden deeper inside our bodies, and they are also busy helping us to survive.

PERFECT PAIR

Muscles make the body move.

Usually, two muscles work to make a movement.

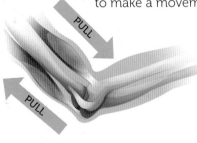

PULL

PULL

One muscle pulls a part of the body one way, then the other muscle in the pair pulls it back the other way.

Muscles do not push.

Muscles are made from many tiny threads of protein. There can be over **10,000 tiny threads** in each muscle!

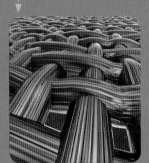

These threads have two important substances called **actin** and **myosin.**

Actin and myosin work together to either **contract** (shorten) or **relax** (extend) muscles.

Here are 10 of the best-known muscles:

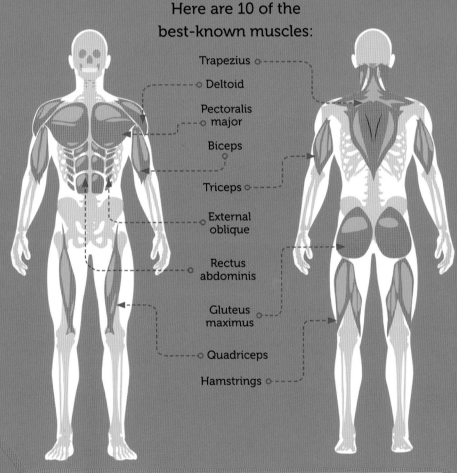

- Trapezius
- Deltoid
- Pectoralis major
- Biceps
- Triceps
- External oblique
- Rectus abdominis
- Gluteus maximus
- Quadriceps
- Hamstrings

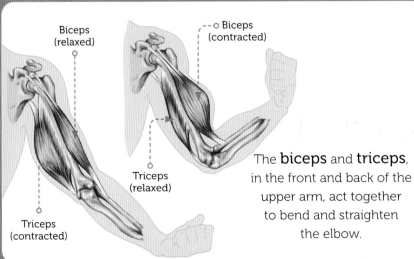

Biceps (relaxed)

Biceps (contracted)

Triceps (relaxed)

Triceps (contracted)

The **biceps** and **triceps**, in the front and back of the upper arm, act together to bend and straighten the elbow.

There are
three types of muscles—
skeletal muscle, smooth muscle, and cardiac muscle.

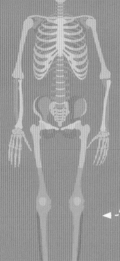

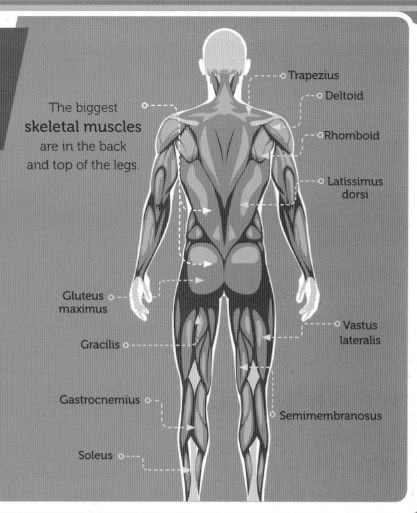

The biggest
skeletal muscles
are in the back
and top of the legs.

- Trapezius
- Deltoid
- Rhomboid
- Latissimus dorsi
- Vastus lateralis
- Semimembranosus

Gluteus maximus

Gracilis

Gastrocnemius

Soleus

Your body has about
640
skeletal muscles.
They make up
approximately
40%
of a human's
total body weight.

Skeletal muscles
are attached to the skeleton in
two or more places.

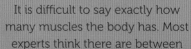

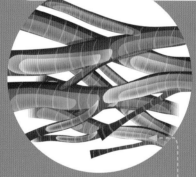

Cardiac muscle
is also a type of involuntary muscle. It
contracts and relaxes within
the heart to help pump blood.

Smooth muscles
are muscles you don't control. They can be known as
involuntary muscles.
Their actions happen without you having to think about it.

3 things smooth muscles can do:

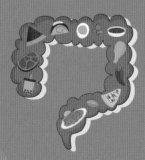

It is difficult to say exactly how
many muscles the body has. Most
experts think there are between
650 and 850.

Counting muscles is tricky because
they are often paired together
and it is hard to identify each one.

1. Move food
through the body.

2. Control the bladder
when you go to the toilet.

3. Help keep
eyes focused.

Eye muscles become tired very easily.
The eyes make about **10,000** movements
during 1 hour of reading!

THE JOB OF JOINTS

Without joints to connect them, bones couldn't do very much. Joints allow the skeleton to bend and move in different directions—and that's how our arms, legs, and fingers do ordinary, everyday things.

A **joint is where two bones meet.** You can easily see them working in your knees, elbows, fingers, and toes—but there are joints all over your body.

Joints hold the **skeleton's bones together** and help it **move and twist in different directions.**

There are **360 joints** in the human body.

We have two types of muscles that make a joint work.

FLEXOR muscles bend a joint and move its connected bone.

EXTENSOR muscles straighten a joint.

The **biceps** muscle in the front of the arm is a **flexor** muscle. The **triceps** in the back of the arm is an **extensor** muscle.

If a person is **too heavy, the extra weight puts more pressure** on joints at their knees, hips, and feet. This can make moving **difficult and painful.**

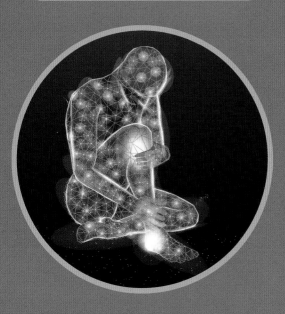

For every **0.45 kg (1 lb)** that someone is overweight, another **1.8 kg (4 lb)** of force can be put on joints.

There are seven kinds of joints:

1

The hip joint and shoulder joint are called **ball-and-socket joints**.

The round top of one bone fits into a shape like a bowl, on another bone.

Ball-and-socket joints enable lots of movement, but they can be **unstable**. If a joint is knocked out of position, it is called a **dislocation**.

2

Wrists and ankles contain **gliding joints**. These are joints where two flat bones glide and slide across each other in any direction.

3

Hinge joints are found in the knee, elbow, and fingers. This type of joint enables a swinging movement in one main direction.

The joint works like a hinge that opens a door or window.

4

The neck and elbow have **pivot joints**. A pivot joint in your neck lets your head move from **side to side**.

Most people can turn their neck only about 80 degrees to the right and 80 degrees to the left.

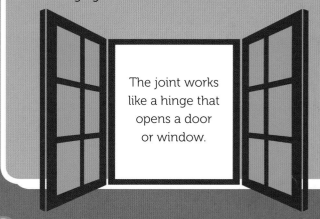

5

The **only saddle joint** in the body is in the base of the thumb. A saddle joint can move easily from side to side, which makes picking things up with the thumb and fingers easier.

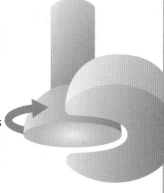

6

Some joints are called **fixed joints**. These give bones strength but do not allow for movement. Fixed joints are in the skull, pelvis (top of the legs), and lower arm.

7

Condyloid joints are found in the wrist, fingers, and toes.

These bend, extend, and rock from side to side, but don't move easily in a circular motion.

51

MAKING A CONNECTION

Think of ligaments, tendons, and cartilage as three friends who all help us to move. Together they make the connections between our bones and muscles, but each one does a different thing!

LOVE YOUR LIGAMENTS

Ligaments
are strong, stretchy tissue around a joint, where **two bones connect**.

A ligament works like a **piece of rope**, with cords wrapped round it to make connecting bones stronger.

Ligaments connect bone to bone and do **four** things:

1. **Keep the joint secure**

2. **Keep the joint from moving too much**

3. **Absorb shock to protect the joint**

4. **Help the body move**

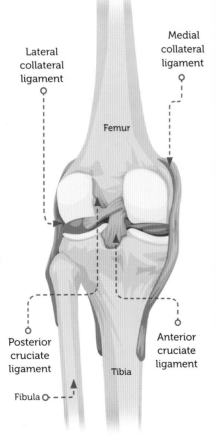

Lateral collateral ligament

Medial collateral ligament

Femur

Posterior cruciate ligament

Anterior cruciate ligament

Tibia

Fibula

The knee has
four major ligaments
that help it move.
They connect the thigh bone (femur) in the upper leg to the shinbone (tibia) in the lower leg.

There are around
900 ligaments in the body.

The neck and head have **70 ligaments**.

There are about **230 ligaments** in the chest, back, and stomach area.

The arms and legs have the most ligaments, with approximately **600**.

Knee ligament damage is a common sports injury.

Sports that need lots of twisting and jumping, such as **basketball, netball,** and **soccer,** risk injury to **knee ligaments**.

Between most bones, there is a joint filled with a liquid called **synovial fluid**. This fluid acts like **lubricating oil** in a car, and keeps the ends of bones from **rubbing together**.

CARTILAGE CARE

Joints at the end of bones have a rubbery covering called **cartilage.**

Working with **synovial fluid,** cartilage helps to cushion joints. It keeps the **end of bones from wearing away**.

There are **three types of cartilage:** **hyaline, fibro,** and **elastic.** Hyaline is the most common.

About **85% of cartilage is water.** In older people, water makes up only about **75%**.

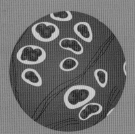
hyaline

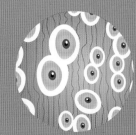
elastic

fibro

The damage to cartilage

can be seen on an **x-ray at a hospital.** If there is a very thin space between 2 bones in a joint, the cartilage has worn away.

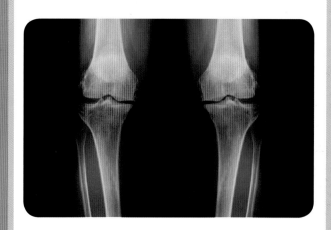

TERRIFIC TENDONS

Tendons are tough tissue which attach muscle to bones.

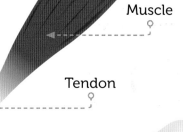
Muscle
Tendon
Bony attachment

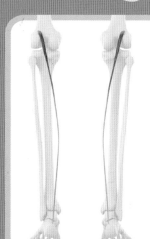

The **longest tendon** is the **plantaris tendon,** which is in the back of the lower leg. In adults it can be **30 cm–45 cm** (12 in–18 in).

LEARN ABOUT LEGS

We use our legs to walk, run, jump, and do many more activities. Leap into learning about the incredible way these long, super-powerful limbs work!

Our legs have **three main jobs:**

1. To support our body weight.

2. To keep us balanced and upright.

3. To move the body.

A leg is made of five parts …

Upper leg (thigh)

Knee

Lower leg

Ankle

Foot

On average, legs make up **50%** **of the height** of an adult.

FEMUR FACTS

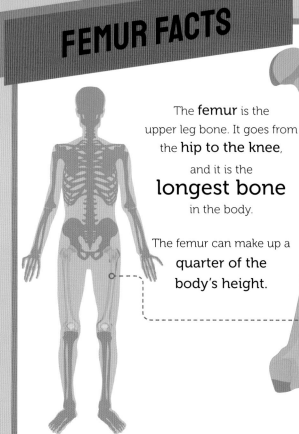

The **femur** is the upper leg bone. It goes from the **hip to the knee,** and it is the **longest bone** in the body.

The femur can make up a **quarter of the body's height.**

The average adult's femur is **48 cm (19 in) long.** That's nearly **$2/3$** the width of a standard door in a house.

Five things the
knee helps the body to do:

walk

run

jump

rotate

pivot

The **bottom (sole) of the foot** has **three arches,** which form a **triangle shape.**

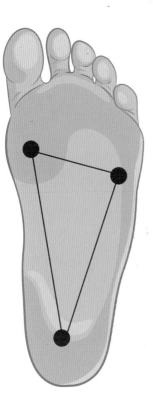

When weight is put on the foot, the **arches flatten to absorb the pressure.** They act a little like **shock absorbers on a car wheel!**

When you run, the pressure on your foot can be **2.5 times greater** than your **body weight.**

The **femur** can support up to **30 times more** than a person's body weight!

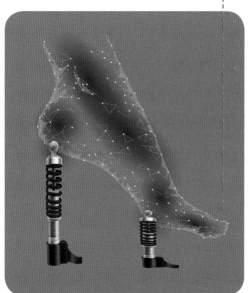

OUT ON A LIMB

Our arms, like our legs, are body parts called limbs. Arms help us lift and carry things—and with their agile hands and nimble fingers, they let us do all kinds of activities, both simple and difficult.

The arm has two parts.

Upper arm

Lower arm

The **upper arm** is from the shoulder to the elbow. The **forearm** is between the elbow and the hand.

BARE BONES

The arm has **three bones**. The **humerus** in the upper arm is a strong bone that gives the arm **power**.

The humerus is very difficult to break. **Only 3%** of all bone breaks happen to the humerus.

The **two bones** in the forearm are the **radius** and **ulna**.

In adults, the radius averages between **22 cm** and **24 cm** (8.6 in and 9.4 in) long.

The ulna is usually between **24 cm** and **27 cm** (9.4 in and 10.6 in) long.

Humerus

Radius

Ulna

The place where the **humerus, radius,** and **ulna** bones meet is the **elbow**. The elbow lets the arm bend and move away from the body.

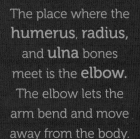

A common injury, where the outer elbow tendons become painful, is called tennis elbow. Tennis elbow can often last between **six months and two years**.

In children, about **40% of broken bones** happen in the forearm.

A child's forearm bones usually heal in **4–6 weeks**.

HANDY NUMBERS

A **human hand** has 27 bones. There are **eight in the wrist, five in the palm, three in each finger**, and **two in the thumb**.

The **thumb is opposable.** which means it moves toward the fingers. This pincer movement helps us pick things up and use tools.

3

2

8

5

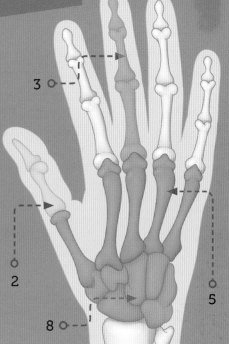

The knuckles in a hand are the ends of the metacarpal bones in the palm.

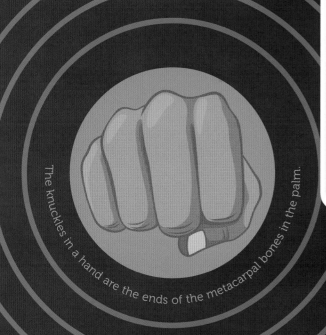

Fingerprints

are on the tip of each finger and thumb. **Every human** has their own fingerprint.

Fingerprints

form when a **baby is still inside the mother's womb**.

Forces moving against the unborn baby's fingers **create the lines and ridges of a fingerprint**.

No **two humans** have been found to have the **same fingerprint**— even **identical twins** have different fingerprints.

The chance that **two people match** is **1 in 64 billion!**

WALK THIS WAY

We walk and run without thinking about it, but our bodies are doing very complicated things when we make these everyday movements. Follow these steps to find out all about it!

BABY STEPS

A baby usually learns to **sit, roll over,** and **crawl** within the first **12 months** of his or her life.

At about **six months old**, the leg muscles are **strong enough** to support the baby's own weight.

Babies often walk by themselves for the first time when they are between **12** and **17** months old.

Walking about **10,000 steps** a day is seen as a good level of activity for an average adult.

MAXIMUM SPEED

The action of walking can be divided into two stages.

The **swing stage** is when one foot is off the ground and the leg is moving (swinging) forward.

The **stance stage** is when the same foot is now on the ground and the leg is supporting the body's weight.

When you walk, **one foot is always** in contact with the ground.

You use around **200 muscles just to walk one step.**

Swing | Stance

The **average walking speed** of an adult is between **4.8** and **6.4 km/h** **(3** and **4 mph).**

FAST FACTS

On your marks, get set ... go!

Running is different to walking because when a person runs, **both feet are off the ground at some stage.**

Gravity force

Vertical force

Horizontal force

When a runner pushes off from the ground with their foot, **three forces act on their body.**

Because **vertical force** is stronger than **gravity force**, the runner can lift off the ground. The **horizontal force** is what moves the runner.

Sprinting is running very fast for a short distance. When an **average person** sprints, each foot is in contact with the ground for just **0.12 seconds.**

When a **professional sprinter** runs, each foot touches the ground for a mere **0.08 seconds.**

How fast can they go?

The best human sprinters can reach a speed of around **40 km/h (25 mph)** on a running track.

A **cheetah** is the **fastest animal**. It can run at around **110 km/h (70 mph)**.

Average man
40 km/h
(25 mph)

Ostrich
70 km/h
(44 mph)

Pig
18 km/h
(11 mph)

GROWING AND CHANGING

The human body's ability to move and be strong depends on healthy growth and development during its lifetime. Older people, who are perhaps not moving so much, may even become a little bit shorter!

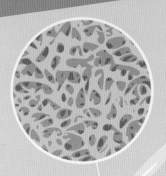

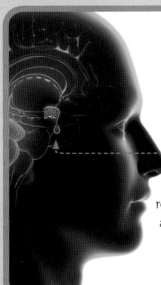

The **pituitary gland** is found at the base of the brain. It releases chemicals that are very important for a child's growth.

Growth hormone from the pituitary **helps bones and other tissues to grow**.

The pituitary is only about **the size of a pea**—but it does a lot!

Chemicals released into the bloodstream by glands are called **hormones.** Some very important hormones are controlled by the pituitary gland:

Prolactin

Growth Hormone

Corticotropin

Antidiuretic hormone

Thyrotropin

Oxytocin

On average, this is how much children grow each year:

1–2 years old:
13 cm (5 in)

3–13 years old:
5 cm (2 in)

2–3 years old:
9 cm (3.5 in)

The average height of adults **varies in different countries.** But, the average across the world for a man born in 1996 is **171 cm (5 ft 6 in)**, and the average height for a woman is **159 cm (5 ft 2 in)**.

The tallest average male height is in the Netherlands, Europe, at **171 cm (5 ft 10 in)**.

The shortest average male height is in Timor-Leste, Southeast Asia, at **160 cm (5 ft 3 in)**.

The shortest average female height is in Guatemala, Central America, at **149 cm (4 ft 9 in)**.

The tallest average female height is in Latvia, Europe, at **169 cm (5 ft 5 in)**.

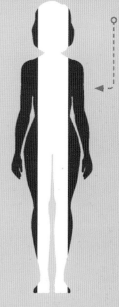

The body shrinks a little as it gets older.

Men can lose about **2.5 cm (1 in)** in height between the ages of **30 to 70**. Women can lose around **5 cm (2 in)**.

Height loss is caused by two things— cartilage between bones wears out, and the spine loses some of its tissue.

The **tallest known human** was Robert Wadlow, who was a towering **272 cm (8 ft 11 in)**. That's about **1 m (3.2 ft) taller** than a baby giraffe!

THE FORCE OF FITNESS

Everybody's body needs regular exercise and activity to help it stay healthy and work properly. Find out exactly what fantastic fitness means for you!

EPIC EXERCISE

The five main benefits of exercise:

1. Stronger muscles
Lifting exercises make muscle cells contract, and that makes them **stronger** and **bigger.**

2. Stronger bones
Exercise that involves moving around, like tennis, dancing, and walking, helps make **strong tissue** inside bones.

3. Less chance of being overweight
Exercise burns up calories, which is the energy we get from food and drink. Too many calories can make the body **overweight.**

4. Lower chance of illness
For example, less unwanted body fat means the **pancreas** has a better chance of controlling a chemical called **insulin**— reducing our risk of type 2 diabetes.

5. Less likely to have high blood pressure
High blood pressure puts stress on organs such as the **heart, kidneys, and brain.** Exercise also helps make the heart stronger and pump more blood.

Exercise that increases our **heart rate** (the speed at which it beats) is particularly good for the heart.

During activity, **we breathe faster** and **take in more oxygen.** The **heart** pumps more **blood** around the body.

There are three main types of exercise:

Endurance exercise, like running and swimming.

Strength exercise, such as weightlifting and push-ups.

Flexibility exercise, including yoga and gymnastics.

Health experts say that the average child between 5 and 18 years old should **exercise for around 60 minutes each day.**

Some sports and activities can combine all **three of the exercise types. Swimming** is a good example of this.

This could be **walking** or **cycling** to school, **activities in the playground,** or **after-school sports** such as tennis or hockey.

When a person exercises, their body releases chemicals called **endorphins,** which make them feel good. So, **happiness** is another benefit of regular exercise.

The average adult should have between **20 and 25 minutes of exercise each day.**

SLEEP TALKING

We need to move around to stay healthy—exercising and finding food are essential for our survival. But we also need to stop and sleep every day. Sleep recharges our batteries—it prepares us for the next day's activities.

Scientists are not totally sure why the body needs sleep, but we know sleep enables us **to recover and rest.**

Hours of sleep

Babies can sleep for **14–15 hours** a day.

Children between 5 and 13 years old may sleep for around **10–12 hours** a day.

Adults often only sleep for about **7–8 hours** a day.

15

10

5

5   10   15   20

Years of age

In comparison, a koala bear can sleep for **18 hours** a day!

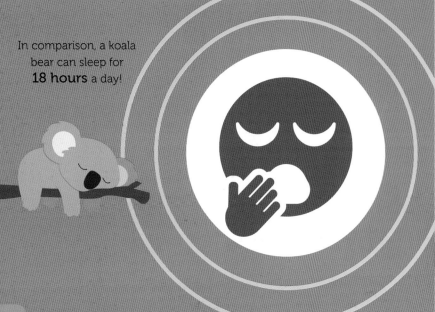

SNOOZE OR LOSE

Sleep is **very important for the brain** to sort out connections it has made and things it has learned.

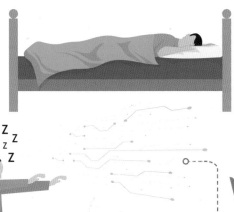

The brain also clears any **waste and unwanted information** while the body sleeps.

If a person misses **one night's sleep,** they will feel **bad-tempered and clumsy.**

After missing **two nights of sleep,** they will struggle to **think properly.**

Going for **five nights without sleep** could make someone see things that are **not really there!**

FOOD FOR THOUGHT

Some foods and drinks are rich in chemicals that help us fall asleep at the end of the day.

Nuts are packed with tryptophan, which helps the brain make sleep-inducing chemicals like serotonin and melatonin.

Milk also contains tryptophan. Having a milky drink may make you feel sleepy and relaxed.

Bananas are high in potassium and magnesium, which help our muscles relax.

When we sleep, the walls of the **throat relax and narrow.** This can lead to **snoring.**

Snoring can be as loud as 80 decibels,
which is about as noisy as a vacuum cleaner!

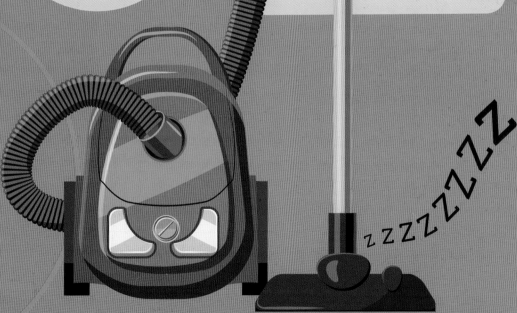

ZZZZZZZZ

PUMP IT UP!

Every second of the day, various parts of the body are busy pumping, beating, expanding, and contracting. The inside of a human is like a building site mixed with a chemical factory—there is always stuff being moved, created, fixed, and sorted!

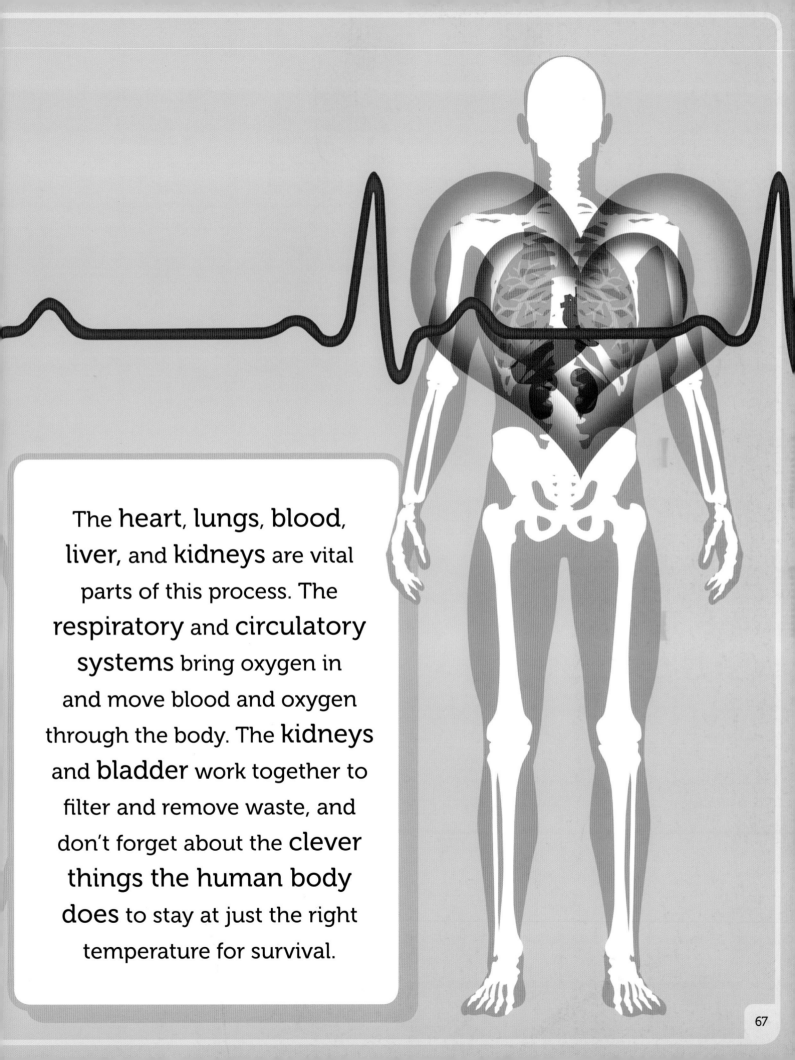

The heart, lungs, blood, liver, and kidneys are vital parts of this process. The respiratory and circulatory systems bring oxygen in and move blood and oxygen through the body. The kidneys and bladder work together to filter and remove waste, and don't forget about the clever things the human body does to stay at just the right temperature for survival.

THE HEART IS A HERO

The heart is a superstar organ that's a real lifesaver! It pumps blood around the body to keep cells healthy and working, and it's just as essential as the brain and lungs for the body's survival.

The heart is both an **organ** and a **muscle**. It is constantly beating, sending blood to every part of the body.

The heart is the star of the **circulatory system** which moves blood carrying oxygen, carbon dioxide, and nutrients (food) around the body.

The left side of the heart pumps blood **rich in oxygen to the body**.
The right side sends blood with **less oxygen to the lungs**.

Blood passes through **four chambers** in the heart. The chambers on the right and left sides are separated by a wall called the **septum**.

Each side has two connected chambers, an **atrium** and a **ventricle**.

Valves in the heart open to let blood move forward, and close quickly to keep it from flowing back.

Blood vessels called **arteries and veins** are connected to the heart. Arteries take blood away from the heart, and veins bring it back.

Superior vena cava

Aorta (to body)

Pulmonary artery (to lung)

Pulmonary veins (from lung)

Right atrium

Left atrium

Left ventricle

Septum

Right ventricle

Inferior vena cava

The **vena cavae** carry oxygen-poor blood from the body to the heart. The **pulmonary artery** takes it from the heart to the lungs.

The **pulmonary veins** return oxygen-rich blood from the lungs to the heart. The **aorta** takes it from the heart back to the body.

BEAT IT

The heart beats between
60 and 100
times a minute,
with an average of around 70 times a minute.
Signals from the brain affect how quickly the
heart beats.

It beats **less** during **sleep and rest**, when
the body **doesn't need** as much **energy**,
so less oxygen is needed in the cells.

During exercise when **more energy** and
oxygen is needed, the heart beats **faster** to
pump more blood.

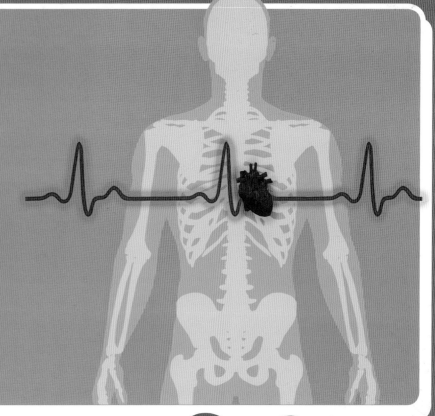

Different creatures have
different heart rates.

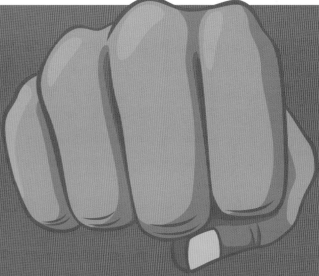

A tiny shrew's heart can beat up to 1,500 times a minute.

A giant blue whale can
have a heartbeat of
just 8 per minute!

The heart is roughly the size of a fist and sits in the
middle of the chest, slightly to the left. On average,
it is around **11 cm (4.3 in)** long, **8.5 cm (3.4 in)**
wide, and weighs about **300 g (0.6 lb)**.

ESSENTIAL BLOOD

That red stuff flowing inside your body is packed with fascinating things! One tiny drop of blood has cells, nutrients, hormones, plasma, and other infection-busting ingredients essential for survival.

Blood does lots of incredible things:

keeps the body warm or cool

helps to fight infections in the body

sends carbon dioxide and waste to the lungs, kidneys, and digestive system

takes oxygen and nutrients to every part of the body

- Plasma makes up approximately **55%** of blood.
- Red blood cells are about **41%** of blood.
- White blood cells make up around **4%** of blood.
- Platelets make up a tiny part of blood, at just **0.001%**.

IN THE MIX

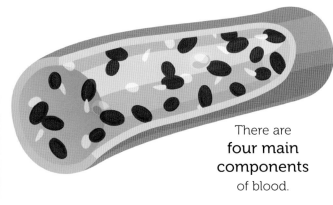

There are **four main components** of blood.

Plasma is a yellowy, liquid substance. It is like a transportation system that carries blood cells, nutrients, hormones, proteins, and waste material along our veins, arteries, and capillaries.

Red blood cells carry oxygen. These cells are what make blood red. Red blood cells live for about four months, and the body makes around

200 billion every day!

White blood cells fight infections caused by germs such as viruses and bacteria. These cells can last for just a few minutes or many years.

Platelets are cells that make a blood clot to repair breaks in blood vessels. Platelets last for around nine days in the bloodstream before being replaced.

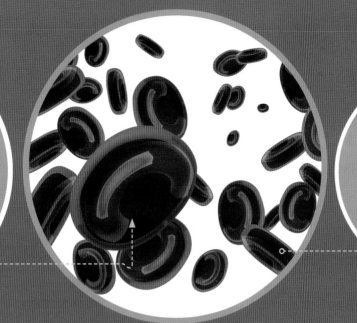

Red blood cells are shaped like flattened disks. This gives them more surface to absorb oxygen and helps them fit through narrow blood vessels.

They have thin walls, called membranes, so oxygen easily reaches the middle of the cell.

The average adult has
4.7 l (159 fl oz) of blood
in their body. Blood is approximately **9%** of a person's body weight.

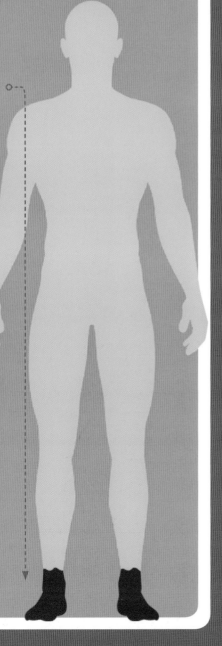

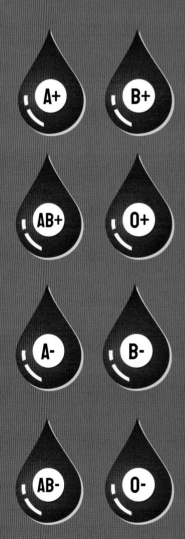

A+   B+

AB+   O+

A-   B-

AB-   O-

Human blood is divided into **eight main groups**. A blood group called "O positive" is generally the most common around the world.

BREATHTAKING LUNGS

The lungs fill up with air to supply oxygen to the body. This pair of awesome organs is the hub of the body's all-important respiratory system.

The body has **two lungs,** but they are not the same size. The **left lung is a little smaller** to leave a space for the heart.

The left lung has **two sections** called lobes, and the right has **three.**

The **trachea** (windpipe) branches into **two bronchi.** Each bronchus branches out into tiny tubes called **bronchioles** inside the lung.

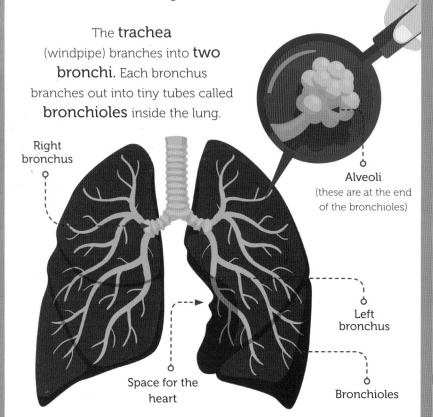

Right bronchus

Alveoli
(these are at the end of the bronchioles)

Left bronchus

Space for the heart

Bronchioles

There are about **30,000 bronchioles in each lung.** The bronchioles end in air sacs called **alveoli.** The body has about **600 million** in the lungs!

Alveoli fill with air when we breathe, letting oxygen pass through their walls into **millions of capillaries** (tiny blood vessels).

Together, the **trachea, bronchi, and bronchioles** are sometimes called the **bronchial tree**—because they look a little bit like a tree and its roots!

The lungs are **so important** that they need protection. They are surrounded by the **rib cage,** which has **12 pairs of ribs.**

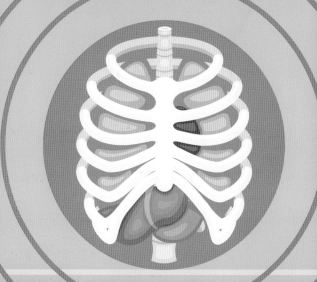

A thin membrane around the lungs, inside the ribcage, is the **pleura**.

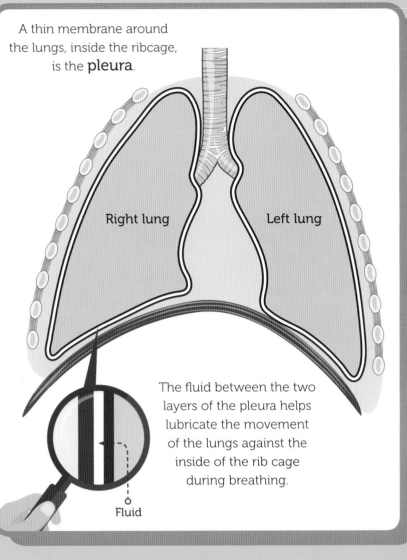

Right lung

Left lung

The fluid between the two layers of the pleura helps lubricate the movement of the lungs against the inside of the rib cage during breathing.

Fluid

The **maximum volume the lungs** can breathe in is about **6 l** (**202 fl oz**). Some highly-trained athletes can increase their lung capacity to between **7** and **8 l** (**237** and **270 fl oz**).

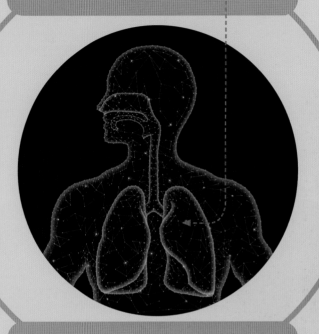

When the lungs exhale (breathe out), only **80% of the air within them** leaves the body. Around **20% of the air stays in the lungs.**

The **diaphragm and muscles** between the ribs make the lungs **expand and contract** during breathing. Sometimes, when more breath is needed, other muscles in the **neck, chest, and abdomen** help, too.

Sternocleidomastoid

Pectoralis major

Serratus anterior

Rectus abdominis

INS AND OUTS

Exactly how do the lungs breathe in to gather oxygen from the air and then breathe out to get rid of carbon dioxide? It's time to breeze through the breathing system!

DIAPHRAGM DETAILS

Breathing is helped by the **diaphragm**, a muscle below the lungs and rib cage.

It is shaped a little bit like a dome.

When someone breathes in, the diaphragm contracts and **moves downward toward the stomach.** At the same time, rib cage muscles pull the ribs up and out. This makes the chest bigger so air can come into the lungs.

When the person breathes out, the diaphragm **relaxes and moves up.** This squeezes the chest and lungs, helping to force air out through the mouth and nose.

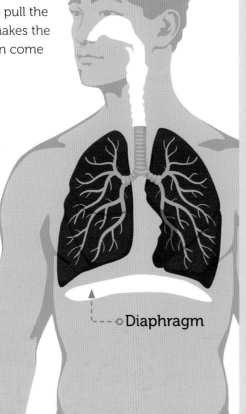

Diaphragm

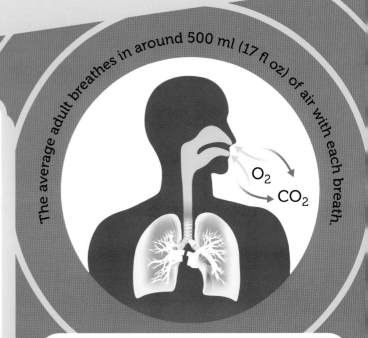

The average adult breathes in around 500 ml (17 fl oz) of air with each breath.

O_2
CO_2

If a human breathes around 16 times a minute, it means they will take about

23,000 breaths a day.

That's 8.5 million breaths a year!

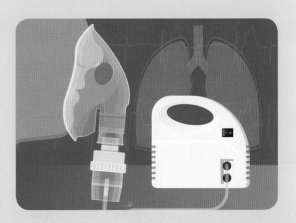

An 80 year old will have taken approximately

673 million breaths

in their lifetime.

Young children breathe much more quickly than adults, at around **40 breaths per minute.**

That's 57,600 breaths a day.

When you **talk, sing, and make sounds,** it's not just the mouth you can thank.

The larynx, at the top of the throat, releases sound from the mouth when you breathe out.

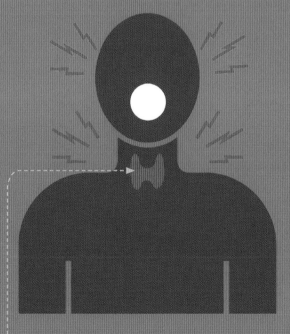

When air leaves the body after breathing in, **vocal cords in the larynx vibrate.**

Another name for the larynx is the voice box.

Some singers' vocal cords vibrate up to **1,000 times a second** when they reach high notes!

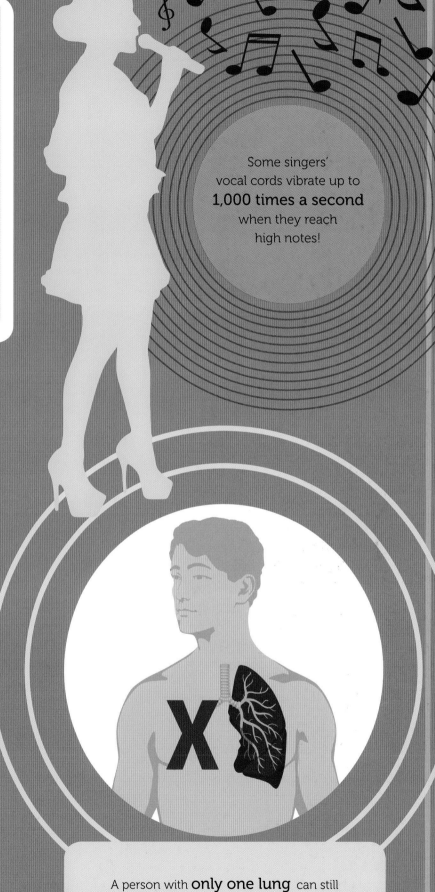

A person with **only one lung** can still breathe in air and survive. Exercising and activity is more difficult though, because less oxygen enters the body.

MOUTH AND NOSE

Essential oxygen enters our lungs when we breathe air in through the mouth and nose. Our bodies have clever ways to keep this system healthy and working well. Face up to the facts on this fascinating page!

We can breathe in through both **nose and mouth**, but breathing with the nose is **better for the body.**

Air passing through the nose is **warmed and filtered for germs** before entering the lungs.

A layer of thin tissue, called **mucous membrane,** warms and adds moisture to the air breathed in.

STOP RIGHT HAIR

The two holes in the nose are **nostrils.** Air enters these and is pulled down into the lungs.

The cells lining the inside of the nasal cavity have microscopic "hair-like" structures called **cilia.** These are covered in a sticky substance called **mucus,** which traps **dust, germs, and dirt.** The cilia collect and move these unwanted particles, ready to be swallowed.

Cilia move dust particles down to the back of the throat.

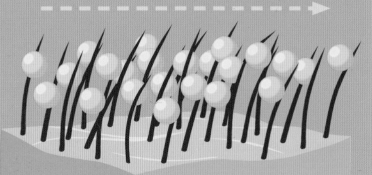

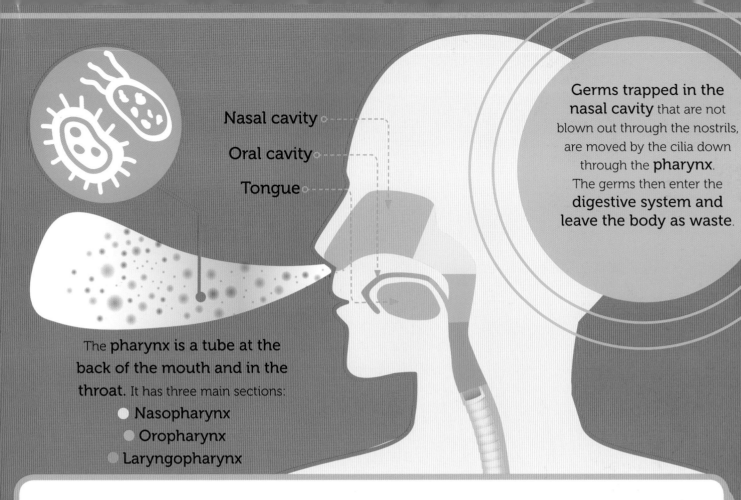

Nasal cavity

Oral cavity

Tongue

Germs trapped in the nasal cavity that are not blown out through the nostrils, are moved by the cilia down through the **pharynx**. The germs then enter the **digestive system and leave the body as waste.**

The **pharynx is a tube at the back of the mouth and in the throat.** It has three main sections:

- Nasopharynx
- Oropharynx
- Laryngopharynx

Breathing through both your **nose** and your **mouth** is the most common way to **inhale (take in) oxygen.** However, when you have a cold, you may find your nose is so blocked that you are unable to breathe through it!

Adults who breathe with their mouth only, and have their mouth open when they sleep may have the following problems:

Snoring
Dry mouth and throat
Tiredness after waking up
Bad breath

Sleeping on your back with your **head raised** on a **high or firm pillow** can help to open the nasal airways and ease breathing through the nose.

LIVE-SAVING LIVER

Your liver is the largest organ in your body and it does lots of important things. Just like the brain and heart, the liver is so special that a human can't live without it.

The **liver** lies mostly on the **right side** of the body's **abdominal area**.
It is above the stomach, right kidney, and intestines, and behind the ribs.

Think of the liver as a **chemical factory**. It changes your **food into energy** you can use and **helps get rid of dangerous substances**.

The busy liver has lots of clever jobs to do:

The liver has three main jobs:

1. To clean and remove harmful things from the blood.

2. To make a liquid called bile, for the digestive system.

3. To store glycogen, which is a substance for storing food energy.

To Do List

☑ Store iron
☑ Remove damaged red blood cells
☑ Help with blood clotting
☑ Make cholesterol
☑ Help medicines heal the body

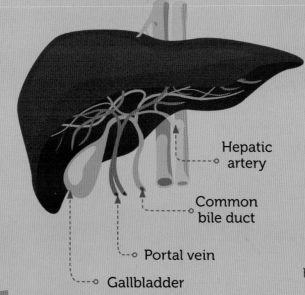

Blood packed with oxygen flows into the liver through the **hepatic artery** directly from your heart.

Blood full of nutrients enters the liver from the intestines through the **portal vein.** Once filtered by the liver, it is transported to your heart.

The liver makes a yellowy-green **fluid called bile.** It makes about **1 l (34 fl oz) a day.**

Hepatic artery

Common bile duct

Portal vein

Gallbladder

Bile is stored in the **gallbladder.** When you eat, bile goes to your intestine, to help **break down fats** in food.

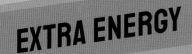

EXTRA ENERGY

The liver uses **carbohydrates** from foods like bread and pasta to give the body energy.

When you need an **energy boost,** the liver breaks down **glycogen** from **carbohydrates** to **release glucose into your blood.**

The liver is **so clever** that even if **75%** of it is damaged, it can rebuild itself and become **a healthy, fully working organ again!**

WELL WATERED

Drinking lots of water every day is a good way to **keep the liver healthy.** Eating healthy food and exercising also means that the liver has less chance of **suffering from disease.**

A sign that the liver is not working well is an illness called jaundice. It makes the skin and eyes look yellow.

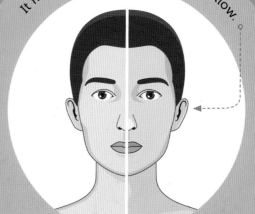

KIDNEYS: FANTASTIC FILTERS

Many people do not know where our kidneys are, but everyone should know the vital work they do! Here, you can filter out the facts and stats of these impressive organs.

Humans have two kidneys.

They are at the back of the abdomen, behind the intestines.

The body can **survive** perfectly well with only **one kidney**.

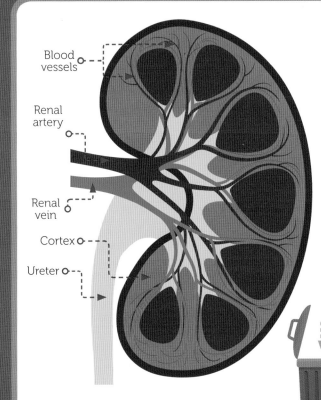

Blood vessels

Renal artery

Renal vein

Cortex

Ureter

The **renal artery** brings blood into the **kidney,** and the **renal vein** takes the **filtered blood away**.

Urine flows down the kidney's **ureter** to the **bladder** and leaves the body. Each kidney has its own ureter.

The main thing that a pair of kidneys does is **filter the body's blood to take waste away.**

Each kidney is about *the size of a phone,* approximately 8 cm (3 in) wide and 13 cm (5 in) long.

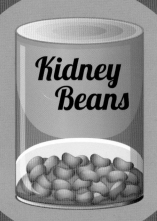

Kidney Beans

A red kidney bean gives you an idea of its shape. They are called kidney beans because they **look like our kidneys!**

24 HOURS IN THE KIDNEYS

On average, an adult has **4.7 l (10 US pints)** of blood in their body. The kidneys filter all of this blood about **30 to 40 times every day!**

Over **150 l (317 US pints)** are checked by the kidneys **in 24 hours.**

Cleaned blood is sent back into the blood system

Each kidney has over **1 million** microscopic filters called **nephrons.**

Nephrons filter the blood to take out waste and water that the body does not need. This **waste** makes **urine** (pee).

Blood enters the kidneys

150 l
(317 US pints)

Nephrons

About **95%** of a person's pee is water.

About **5%** is waste.

1.5 l
(3 US pints)

The body can make **1.5 l (3 US pints)** of pee a day.

The kidneys help to **balance the amount of water in the body.** If the body needs to keep more water, the brain sends a message to the kidneys to release less water through pee.

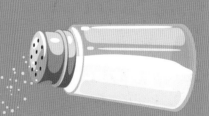

The kidneys balance the levels of **salts** in the blood and remove wastes. The main waste is called **urea.**

BLADDER

Along with the kidneys, the bladder is an important part of a human's urinary system—the system that removes waste as pee. Discover more about this important bodily function.

Pee (urine) collects in an area at the bottom of the abdomen, called the **bladder**.

It arrives in the **bladder through two tubes called ureters.** Each ureter is about 24–30 cm (9–12 in) long.

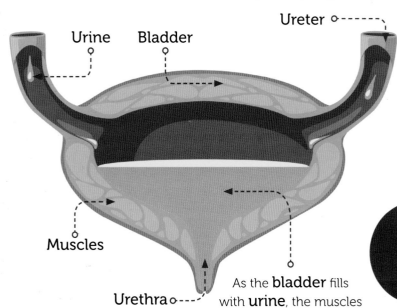

Urine   Bladder   Ureter

Muscles

Urethra

As the **bladder** fills with **urine**, the muscles expand and stretch to hold the liquid.

When the bladder is about **50% full,** nerves send a message to the brain that you **need to go to the bathroom.**

The **bladder muscles then contract** (squeeze) to **push urine out through the urethra.**

Muscles around the **urethra relax,** and it opens so that **pee can be released.**

Babies can't **control their urethra.** They can't usually go to the toilet by themselves until they are around **two years** old.

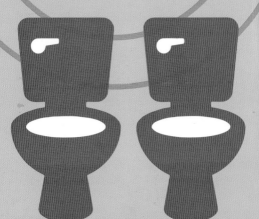

An adult's bladder can usually hold about

500–600 ml (17–20 fl oz)

without feeling the need to rush to the toilet.

The **shade of your pee** tells you if you have been drinking enough water. A dark yellow shade means you **need to drink more liquids!**

TRANSPARENT
You're drinking a lot of water

PALE
Normal drinking

LIGHT YELLOW
You need to drink more water

DARK YELLOW
Drink a lot more water!

People drinking a normal amount of water may pee about **seven times a day on average.** **That is over 2,500 times a year!**

TAKE THE TEMPERATURE

We can suffer badly if we become too hot or too cold, so controlling temperature is one of the most important things the human body does. Blood plays a big part in this life-saving heating and cooling system.

HOT STUFF

We are most comfortable with a **body temperature of 37° C (98.6° F).**

At this temperature, the human body is warm enough to beat infections. It also doesn't need too much food to keep energy levels high.

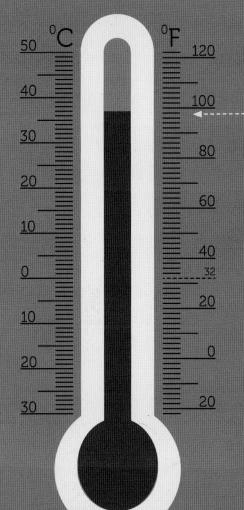

SIGNS OF DEHYDRATION

If body temperature rises above **37° C (98.6° F)**, it can cause a harmful loss of water called **dehydration.**

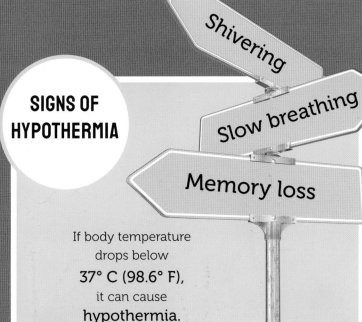

Very thirsty

Tired or sleepy

Headache and dizziness

SIGNS OF HYPOTHERMIA

Shivering

Slow breathing

Memory loss

If body temperature drops below **37° C (98.6° F)**, it can cause **hypothermia.** This is when the body loses more heat than it creates.

COOL SYSTEM

The flow of blood to the skin's surface **helps cool body temperature.**

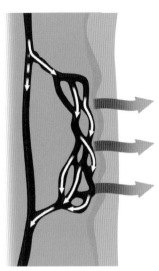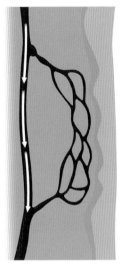

The blood releases heat through the skin

The blood keeps heat inside the body

When **blood vessels expand,** warm blood goes to the surface and heat is lost into the air. **This is vasodilation.**

The opposite of vasodilation is **vasoconstriction.** When vasoconstriction happens, **less blood reaches the skin surface** and less heat is lost.

SWEAT IT OUT

Human **skin** is covered in **sweat glands.** When the body is hot, they send sweat to the skin's surface.

Sweat is a salty liquid.

When sweat evaporates from the surface, **it cools the body down.**

A human body has roughly between **2** and **4 million sweat glands!**

HAIR AND HEAT

Shivering happens automatically when you get cold. Messages from the brain make your muscles shake.

Shaking and movement makes heat, which is then pumped around in the blood to warm you up.

Your body's **ability to control** its **temperature** is called **thermoregulation.**

Body hair plays a role in controlling temperature.

When the body is cold, **skin muscles pull hairs upright.** The hairs can then trap warm air.

If the body gets too warm, the **hair muscles relax.** This makes hair lie flat and lets heat escape.

HEALTHY APPETITE

Feeling hungry?
Before you load up your
fork, take a minute to think
about what happens to all that
food when it enters your body
and **how long it takes to come
out of the other end!**
The human digestive system begins in the
mouth with **chewing** and **swallowing**,
and it ends with a visit
to the bathroom for waste removal!

Food travels a long way during the digestive process. It passes through organs, such as the stomach and intestines, where it's mashed up and broken down.

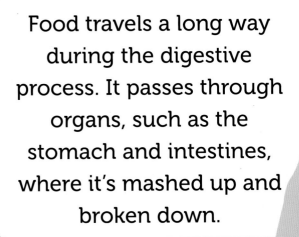

The good parts of food are used to help our bodies grow and stay healthy. We need to eat a diet balanced with different types of food, from fruit and vegetables to energy-packed pasta and rice. Read on for a tasty trip along the digestive system!

TELL THE TOOTH

We need to eat food to give us energy to move and stay healthy. The start of the process is biting and chewing—and our teeth are just the thing to do this very well!

The **first teeth** appear when a baby is between **6** and **12 months old**. These are often called **milk teeth**.

Teeth grow through the gum, which is the soft pink part in the mouth. **Gums hold teeth in place.**

The white part of the tooth, above the gum, **is the crown.** It is covered in shiny, hard enamel.

By the time a **child is three,** they usually have all
20 milk teeth.

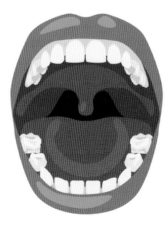

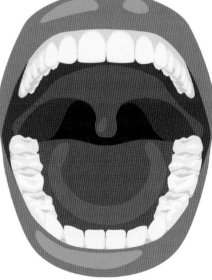

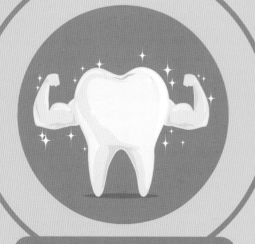

Enamel is the toughest substance in the body. It protects the inner part of a tooth.

If tooth enamel is lost, it can't be replaced.

By the time a child is **five or six years** old, the milk teeth **start to fall out** and are replaced by **adult teeth.** At 12–14, children usually have all their adult teeth.

Adults have 32 teeth.

If these fall out or are knocked out accidentally, the body does not replace them.

Dentists say that teeth should be brushed with toothpaste two times a day for between 2 and 3 minutes each time.

Sugary food and drinks help the growth of **bacteria** in the mouth. This builds up into a sticky layer, called **plaque,** on the teeth.

The bacteria produce **acid,** which dissolves tooth enamel and can make holes (cavities) in your teeth. **Cavities** can be repaired by the dentist.

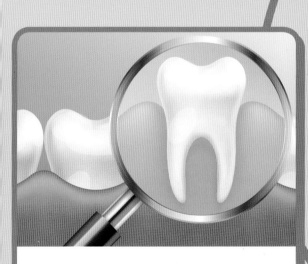

The **root part of a tooth** is under the gum. It makes up about $2/3$ **the size of** the tooth.

CHEW OVER THE FACTS

Digestion starts in the mouth, where the teeth and tongue help to chew food up. Once chewed, it can be swallowed and begin its journey through the stomach and intestines.

Adults have four types of teeth.

Each type has a different job to help with **cutting and chewing food.**

1. **Incisors** are the four teeth at the front of the top and bottom jaw. **They cut and chop food.**

2. The four **canine** teeth are on each side of the incisors. **They are sharp and tear food.**

3. **Premolars crush and grind food.** There are four on the top and four on the bottom of the jaw, next to the canine teeth.

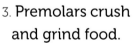

4. The **molars**, at the back of the jaw, are the **strongest teeth.** These 12 teeth work with the tongue to **mash food to prepare it for swallowing.**

FAST FACTS

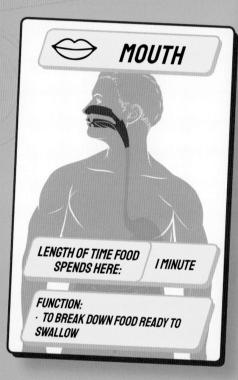

MOUTH

LENGTH OF TIME FOOD SPENDS HERE: | I MINUTE

FUNCTION:
· TO BREAK DOWN FOOD READY TO SWALLOW

Humans are omnivores, which means we can **eat plants and meat.** Molar teeth grind plant food, and incisors and canines rip and cut meat, ready for digestion.

Meat-eating carnivore animals, such as tigers, mainly use their powerful canine and incisor teeth.

The mouth produces a watery liquid called **saliva.** This contains chemicals (enzymes) that help break food down even further.

There are three types of glands that make saliva:

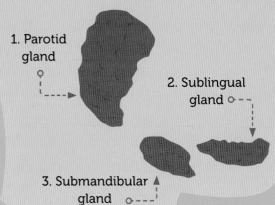

1. Parotid gland

2. Sublingual gland

3. Submandibular gland

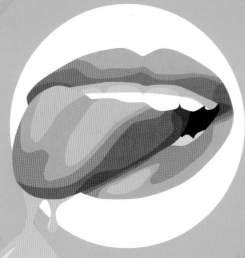

The body can make between **1 and 2 l (34 and 68 fl oz)** of saliva every day!

There are **four main muscles** in the mouth and head that help chew food:

1. Masseter muscle
2. Temporalis muscle
3. Medial pterygoid muscle
4. Lateral pterygoid muscle

Experts say **food should be chewed an average of 32 times** before swallowing.

32

Food like **steak** and **nuts** need around **40 chews.**

Softer food, such as **watermelon,** could need only **10 chews.**

The tongue does **two jobs to help digestion:**

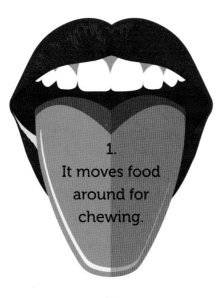

1. It moves food around for chewing.

2. It pushes small bits of food to the back of the mouth, ready to be swallowed.

PIPE DOWN

When we swallow chewed-up food, it makes a quick journey down to the stomach. The food pipe is the body part that takes it on this tasty trip!

BLOCKING OFF

The **mouth** is used for both **breathing in air** and for **swallowing food**. It could be dangerous if food got into the lungs. Luckily, the human body has clever ways to stop a mix-up!

A piece of skin behind the tongue called the **epiglottis** keeps food from going down the **windpipe**.

When a person swallows food or liquids, the epiglottis closes. This sends the substances down the food pipe **to the stomach** and **not the lungs**.

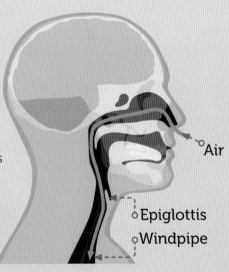

Air
Epiglottis
Windpipe

The epiglottis stays open when a person is not swallowing, so that **air** moves to the lungs.

The **epiglottis** is made from **cartilage**, which is like a **rubbery bone**.

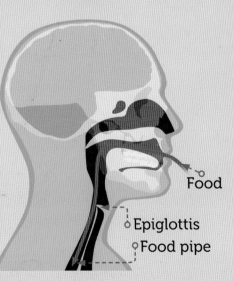

Food
Epiglottis
Food pipe

FAST FACTS

FOOD PIPE

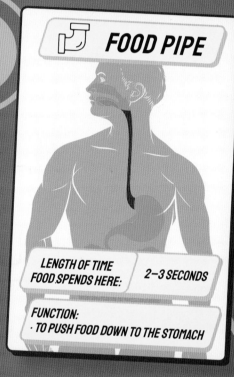

| LENGTH OF TIME FOOD SPENDS HERE: | 2–3 SECONDS |

FUNCTION:
· TO PUSH FOOD DOWN TO THE STOMACH

The **alimentary canal** is the name for the whole of the **digestive system**, starting with the **mouth** and finishing at the **bottom** where waste is released.

Stretched out, the alimentary canal is about
9 m (30 ft).
That's the length of two great white sharks!

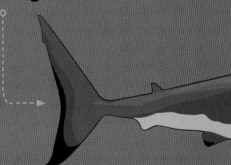

The **food pipe** stretches from the back of the throat to the stomach.

Muscles in the food pipe **squeeze** to **push** food to the **stomach**. This is called **peristalsis**.

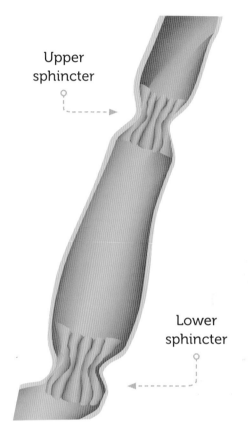

Upper sphincter

Lower sphincter

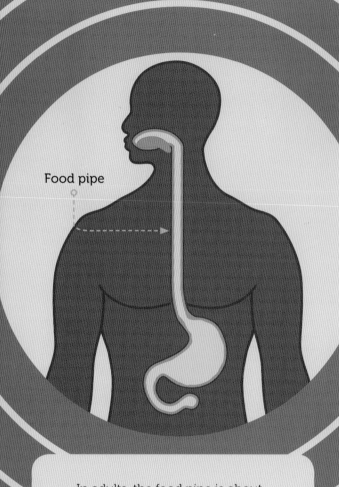

Food pipe

In adults, the food pipe is about **25 cm (10 in) long.** That's a little bit smaller than the distance between the **elbow** and **the wrist.**

There are two muscles called **sphincters** at the top and bottom of the pipe.

These muscles **relax to let food move down.** They tighten again to **keep food and stomach acid from moving back up the pipe.**

30 muscles and **nerves work together** to push food to the stomach.

MIXING AND MASHING

The stomach is a smart part of the body. It uses muscles and acids to break down food. But watch out— it is a little bit stinky and it can make some yucky-smelling gases!

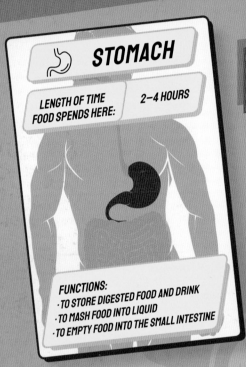

STOMACH

LENGTH OF TIME FOOD SPENDS HERE:	2–4 HOURS

FUNCTIONS:
· TO STORE DIGESTED FOOD AND DRINK
· TO MASH FOOD INTO LIQUID
· TO EMPTY FOOD INTO THE SMALL INTESTINE

GREAT GROWING

A newborn baby's stomach grows very, very quickly ...

At 24 hours old, it is the size of a marble.

At 3 days old, it is the size of a walnut.

At 8–10 days old, it is the size of a golf ball.

FAST FACTS

The **stomach** is found just to the left, in the upper abdominal cavity. It is below the **diaphragm**.

In adults, an empty stomach is about **30 cm (12 in) long and 15 cm (6 in) wide.**

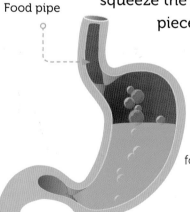

Food pipe

Muscles in the stomach wall squeeze the small, chewed-up pieces of food.

Digestive stomach **juices,** which are full of **acids** and enzymes, churn and break food into even smaller pieces.

All this churning can make **gases,** which the stomach gets rid of as a **burp.** Carbonated drinks **have lots of gases that make us burp!**

People can burp **3–6 times** after a meal.

The stomach acts like a food mixer to mash food and turn it into liquid.

Acids in the stomach are almost as **strong as battery acid,** which can **dissolve some metals!**

The stomach stretches as it fills. When it feels full, nerves send messages to the brain **to stop eating!** **These messages can take up to 20 minutes.**

20 SECONDS

The stomach contracts about **every 20 seconds** to mix up food, so it is very busy. The thick liquid it makes is called **chyme.**

About **2–4 hours** after eating, the food in the **stomach** is emptied.

INTERESTING INTESTINE

They share a name, but the small and large intestines are different parts of the digestive system and do different things. First, find out what a superstar the small intestine is!

The **small intestine** is actually longer than the large intestine! Laid out it is around 6 m (20 ft) long.

That's longer than the height of two Asian elephants.

FAST FACTS

SMALL INTESTINE

LENGTH OF TIME FOOD SPENDS HERE:	4–8 HOURS

FUNCTIONS:
· TO SOAK UP NUTRIENTS FROM DIGESTED FOOD AND TRANSPORT THEM TO THE BLOOD

The **small intestine** is curled up and fits inside the middle of the abdomen. The **large intestine** lies around it.

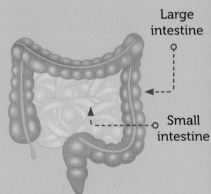

Large intestine

Small intestine

It is called the **"small"** intestine because it is narrower than the large intestine, at **2.5 cm (1 in) wide.**

MEDIUM

LOW

HIGH

ENERGY

The small intestine's job is to **absorb** (soak up) **nutrients** from **digested food** and pass them into the blood to **give the body energy.**

The first part of the **small intestine** needs juices from the **pancreas, liver,** and **gallbladder** to help it digest and absorb nutrients.

Millions and millions of tiny lumps

called **villi** cover the inner walls of the small intestine.

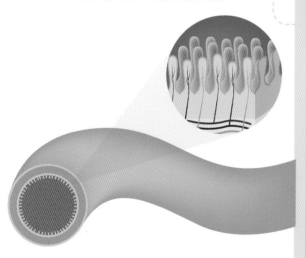

In an area the size of this square in the small intestine, there could be up to **25,000 villi!**

The small intestine has three parts:

1. The duodenum is the first section.

The duodenum is shaped like a C and receives the mushy liquid **chyme from the stomach.**

Stomach

Duodenum

2. The jejunum is in the middle.

3. The ileum is the end section.

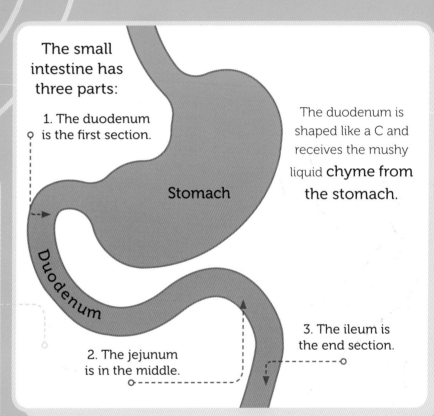

Villi increase the surface size of the small intestine and let nutrients from food pass through them into the bloodstream. **They are like a delivery truck taking goodness to the blood.**

FAST DELIVERY

MOVING ALONG

The large intestine is the last stage of the journey through the digestive system. Here, water is reabsorbed and the final morsels of goodness are taken out from what's left of your food. The remaining intestinal contents are then pushed along to the rectum as waste.

The **large intestine** is wrapped around the small intestine. Stretched out, it is about **1.5 m (5 ft) long,** which is almost the height of the **average female adult.**

The **large intestine** is 7.5 cm (3 in) wide. That's **3 times thicker** than the small intestine.

FAST FACTS

A blue whale can have over **200 m (656 ft) of intestines.** That's roughly **25 times more than a human!**

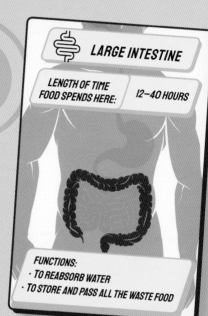

LARGE INTESTINE	
LENGTH OF TIME FOOD SPENDS HERE:	12–40 HOURS

FUNCTIONS:
- TO REABSORB WATER
- TO STORE AND PASS ALL THE WASTE FOOD

The large intestine has several different parts:

- Transverse colon
- Ascending colon
- Appendix
- Descending colon
- Sigmoid colon
- Rectum
- Anus

Muscles in the large intestine **squeeze** and **relax** to slowly force **waste (poop)** along.

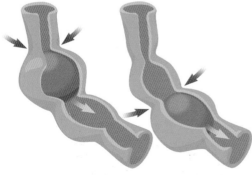

Waste is then stored in the **rectum,** at the end of the large intestine, before a person goes to the bathroom to release it.

Any **mashed-up food** not absorbed into the blood through the small intestine reaches the large intestine.

It is **waste that the body must get rid of.**

Waste can take as long as **40 hours to move through the large intestine.**

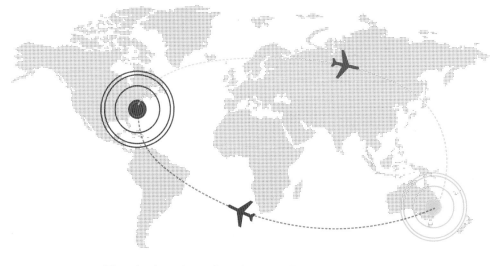

That's the time it takes to fly from New York, USA, to Sydney, Australia, and back again!

Trillions of bacteria in the large intestine break up undigested food to make waste.

Bacteria in the large intestine make vitamins K and B, which are good for the body.

VITAMINS

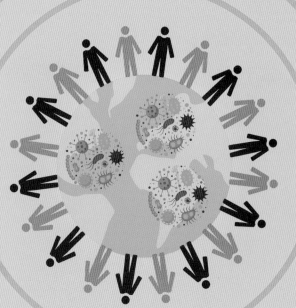

There are more bacteria in the large intestine than there are people in the world!

The large intestine has more than **1,000** different types of bacteria.

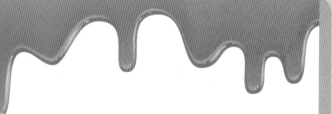

A moist substance called **mucus** is made in the walls of the **intestine**. This helps waste move along. The **mucus** is renewed about every hour.

THE WONDER OF WASTE!

It is a bit yucky, but everybody needs to remove waste every day with a trip to the bathroom! Discover why it is important and what makes it happen.

Some people **poop every day**, others perhaps **4–5 times a week**.

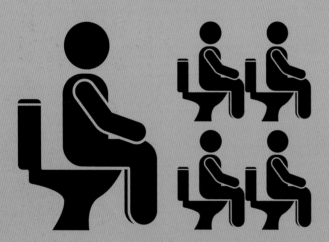

Poop is usually a **shade of brown** but can sometimes be **slightly green** or **yellow**.

It is that shade because of the **food we eat** and because **bile**, a yellowy-green substance made by the **liver**, mixes with our food to break it down.

The three main things that can affect how often a person goes to the toilet are:

1. Diet

Eating foods like vegetables and **fruit** can make it easier for the **body to remove waste**.

2. Age

An older person might have less movement inside their intestines. **Medicines** can also have the effect of slowing down the process of **waste removal**.

3. Activity

Walking and **exercise** help digested food move through the **digestion system**.

GAS LEAK ...

It is estimated that **we all fart between 5 and 15 times a day!**
This is also known as **flatulence** and **intestinal gas.**

Farting is **completely natural and normal.** It is the build-up of **waste gases** being released by the anus (bottom).

The **gases** enter the body through the mouth and nose, and are also made when food is broken down.

These are the **main gases** that make up a fart:

Nitrogen

Hydrogen

Carbon dioxide

Methane

Oxygen

Hydrogen sulfide

Ammonia

The right amount of water needs to be removed from waste before it leaves the body.

If there is too much water in the waste, or too little, pooping can be uncomfortable!

ON THE MENU

To stay healthy, your body needs you to eat a balanced diet of all the right types of food, with lots of variety. Take a look at what should be on the perfect menu!

Nutrients in different foods keep our bodies **strong** and **healthy**. There are **four types of nutrients:**

1. Carbohydrates
They make energy and are in foods like bread, potatoes, rice, and pasta.

2. Lipids
These are **fats** and **oils** in things like fish and butter, which give us energy.

3. Proteins
They make **new cells** and **repair old cells.** Beans, milk, meat, and eggs have lots of protein.

4. Vitamins and minerals
These **help cells** and can **prevent illness.** Broccoli has **vitamins C and K.**

Minerals help the **body grow, make cells work,** and **keep bones and teeth strong.**

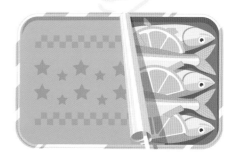

There are **16 essential minerals**, including **calcium, iron,** and **magnesium.** Vegetables, milk, and small fish, such as sardines, are packed with minerals.

Experts say that around **70%** of energy should come from **carbohydrates,** and around **30%** from **fats.**

Experts recommend that we eat plenty of fruit and vegetables each day to stay healthy.

Some types of foods have been called "superfoods," because people claim that they have special powers to keep you healthy. They include **onions, kale, nuts, and salmon.**

These are good for you, but the best thing to keep healthy is to eat a wide variety of different foods.

Small chocolate bar = 103 kcal

Carrot = 35 kcal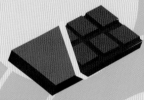

The **average adult female** needs about 2,000 kcal (kilo calories) of energy each day. The **average adult male** needs around 2,500 kcal.

Banana = 100 kcal

200 g (7 oz) beef = 342 kcal

ENERGY BOOST

Our brilliant bodies can do all kinds of energetic activities, but we all feel tired sometimes. This could mean that we need to get more energy from the things we eat and drink.

Every part of the human body needs energy to work.
We get this energy from food.

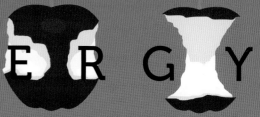

ENERGY TYPES

Our bodies use **digested food** to make a chemical called **adenosine triphosphate (ATP)**. ATP supplies energy for all our cells. There are **three different types of ATP energy:**

1.
ATP-PC
Energy for **high-intensity movements** and **exercises**, such as **sprinting**, lasting for about **10 seconds**.

2.
Aerobic phosphorylation
A **slow-release energy** for activities such as **walking and swimming** that take a longer time.

3.
Anaerobic glycolysis
Energy that powers the body in heavy exercise, such as **boxing**, for **2–3 minutes**.

HUNGER PAIN

The sense of being hungry is controlled by the brain.

When you have used up your last meal, your empty **stomach** sends a signal through the **vagus nerve to the brain.**

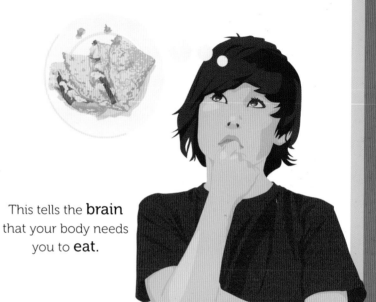

This tells the **brain** that your body needs you to **eat.**

When the body hasn't eaten enough food to turn into energy,

we can feel dizzy, faint, and out of breath.

A chemical called **lactic acid** can make parts of the body **painful during exercise.** It can be a **burning feeling.**

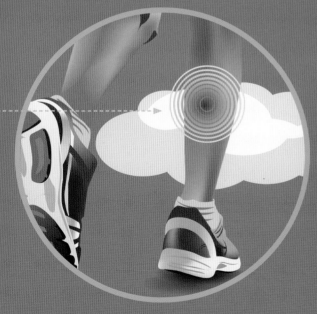

The lactic acid builds up in muscles, because they have been working hard and need to get more oxygen.

Lactic acid goes away when you rest. Certain foods, such as **tomatoes** and **some nuts,** may help.

SICKNESS AND HEALTH

We all know what it's like to feel unwell. Health problems can be simple, like a **cold** or **headache**, or more serious, such as **broken bones** and **breathing difficulties**. Luckily, the human body is very good at **protecting against nasty attacks** and it's surprisingly clever at **repairing itself** if something bad happens.

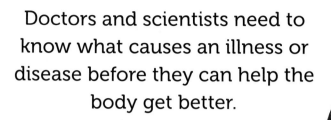

Doctors and scientists need to know what causes an illness or disease before they can help the body get better.

Understanding what causes illnesses means they can choose the best treatments, which might include medicines and operations.

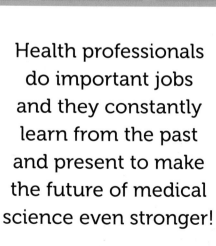

Health professionals do important jobs and they constantly learn from the past and present to make the future of medical science even stronger!

DISEASE AND ILLNESS

Doctors and scientists study what causes disease and illness. They learn how to treat people who get ill, and even how to keep diseases from happening.

DISEASE IN DETAIL

There are four main types of diseases:

1. Infectious diseases
2. Deficiency diseases
3. Hereditary diseases
4. Physiological diseases

A **deficiency disease** is caused when a person does not have enough of a **certain vitamin** or **mineral**.

Infectious diseases are the most common type. They can be passed from **person to person.** The body is **attacked** by **harmful invaders** such as **viruses** and **bacteria.**

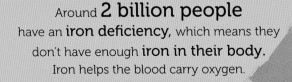

Around **2 billion people** have an **iron deficiency,** which means they don't have enough **iron in their body.** Iron helps the blood carry oxygen.

A **hereditary disease** is passed down through a family from parents to their children. The disease is part of a **person's genes.**

Physiological diseases happen when a part of the body isn't working properly. These include diseases such as **diabetes, cancer,** and **asthma.**

Diabetes is a disease which means that the **pancreas** does not produce enough of a chemical called **insulin.**

Pancreas

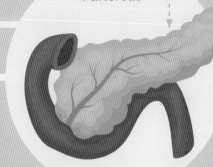

The **World Health Organization** says that the **five types of disease** that cause the most deaths each year are:

1. **Heart disease**

2. **Stroke**
(loss of blood to the brain)

3. **Lung disease**

4. **Lower respiratory infections,**
such as the flu

5. **Dementia**
(problems with the brain working)

In the United States, about **500 million colds** are caught each year. Colds are the most common **infectious disease.**

ATCHOO!

A **doctor** who studies diseases is called a **pathologist.**

A **cold** is an **infection** that affects the nose and throat, and can cause sneezing, a runny nose, and poor breathing.

IMMENSE IMMUNE SYSTEM

The clever immune system is always trying to keep us healthy. We don't notice it working until something happens to us, and the system takes urgent action.

The **immune system** is the body's way of protecting itself from **infections** and **germs** that try to **attack it**. It's like a brick wall that keeps out an enemy!

But the **body has other things that protect it first,** before the immune system even needs to act:

The **skin protects** the body from **germs** and is a barrier that keeps stuff from getting inside.

Stomach acid can **kill germs** that may have come inside through food and drink.

Tiny hairs (cilia) in the lining of the nose **trap** some **germs** before they can get any further.

SUPER CELLS

Microscopic **white blood cells** in the immune system are one of the best ways the body protects against **infections** and **germs**.

These white blood cells are called **leukocytes.**

Leukocytes are made around the body, including in **marrow** inside bones, the **spleen** in the abdomen, and **thymus** in the chest.

There are two types of **leukocytes**— **phagocytes** and **lymphocytes.**

Phagocytes are **hungry cells** that engulf and eat up germs to get rid of them.

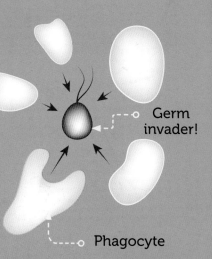

Germ invader!

Phagocyte

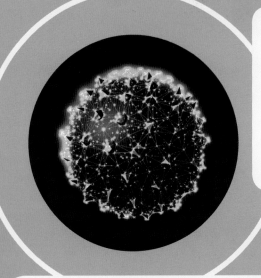

Lymphocytes are cells that remember germs. Some of them make proteins called antibodies, which stay in the body to defend against an illness if it comes back.

If a child has chickenpox, antibodies usually make sure he or she can't catch it again in the future.

If there is a skin infection, a yellowy substance called pus might appear. Pus is dead white blood cells that have beaten the infection.

Lymph nodes are found in lots of places, such as in the armpits, chest, and neck, and behind the knees.

When a mosquito bites skin and injects saliva, white blood cells rush to the bite and attack the infection.

Lymph nodes work like filters to detect and remove harmful germs.

The mix of insect saliva and white blood cells make the bite itchy.

HELPFUL HEALING

The immune system is fantastic at preventing infections, but there are lots of other ways the body can heal. Prepare for some great repair work!

BREAK IT DOWN

Bones are tough but can break (fracture).

Bones might be **completely broken** or just **partly,** which may be called a **hairline fracture.**

The body has **special powers to repair** and **heal bones.**

The **three stages** of bone repair and healing are the **inflammatory stage, reparative stage,** and **rebuilding stage.**

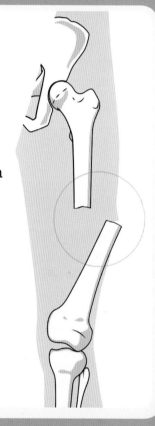

1. Inflammatory stage

About 2–3 hours after a bone is broken, **a blood clot** is made around the bone, causing **swelling.** Blood clots **control bleeding** and help **prevent infection.**

Cells in the blood will also act to **kill germs** and **stop infection.**

2. Reparative stage

New bone tissue, called **collagen,** is created around the fracture. This can last for **1–3 weeks.**

3. Rebuilding stage

New bone is made to **repair the break,** which may take **6–12 weeks.**

It can sometimes take **39 years** for the bone to be **completely healed.**

COMA CARE

If a person is in a **coma**, it means they are **unconscious** and will **not respond to people around them.**

A coma can happen after a **serious injury** to the head and brain.

Sometimes the body's natural healing powers need a little help.

Vaccination is when a **small amount of weakened or dead virus or bacteria** is injected into the body through the skin.

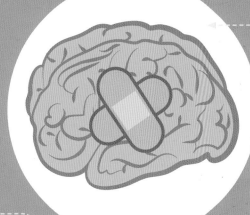

After a head injury, the brain becomes less alert and active. A **coma** is the body's way of **protecting itself** from more damage. A person may be in a **coma** for **days, weeks,** or even **months** before they **wake up** and **recover.**

After a **vaccination,** the body detects the injected virus or bacteria and makes **antibodies** to **defend against** it. So if the **virus or bacteria** does **attack for real,** the body is already **prepared.**

REMARKABLE MEDICINE

If you feel unwell or have an illness, your doctor might give you medicine to help you get better. We have modern medicines to help with many diseases, and they work in lots of different ways.

Medicines are the chemicals we use to stop or slow down an illness.

They can also help with other problems from an illness, such as a sore throat from a cold. This is called a **symptom**.

Medicines are usually made in **laboratories** with **special equipment**. Lots of **medicines** and **drugs** have also come from **plants** and **nature**.

Parts of the **foxglove** were used to make a drug for the heart called **digoxin**.

There are **thousands** of medicines around the world, and many new medicines and drugs are made each year.

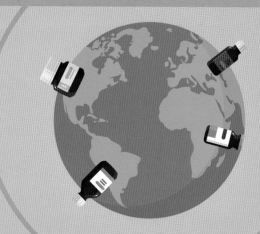

The **World Health Organization** keeps the **Model List of Essential Medicines**. It lists over **400 medicines** that are the most important ones for human health.

MANY MEDICINES

The body can take in medicines in **lots of different ways:**

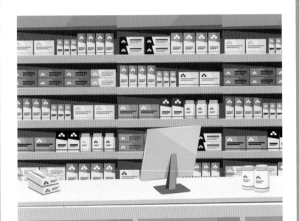

1. **Liquids** and **pills** that at are swallowed
2. **Creams** put on the skin
3. **Patches** attached to the skin
4. **Injections** into the skin
5. **Intravenous** (injected into a vein)
6. **Inhalers** such as masks and sprays

Swallowed medicines mix with juices in the stomach and pass into the **bloodstream.** The blood takes the medicine to where it is needed.

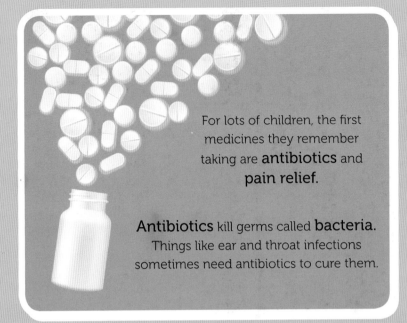

For lots of children, the first medicines they remember taking are **antibiotics** and **pain relief.**

Antibiotics kill germs called **bacteria.** Things like ear and throat infections sometimes need antibiotics to cure them.

PAIN

RELIEF

When a part of the body is in pain, **that part's cells release a chemical called prostaglandin.** This chemical tells the brain all about the pain.

Pain relief medicine, like **ibuprofen,** keeps injured cells from making prostaglandin, so that the **pain messages to the brain stop.**

Hundreds of years ago, **doctors didn't really know what caused illnesses** and which medicines to use.

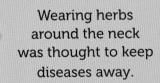

Wearing herbs around the neck was thought to keep diseases away.

In England until the nineteenth century, people incorrectly thought bad smells caused diseases.

DOCTOR, DOCTOR ...

Doctors, nurses, and healthcare workers do some of the most important jobs in the world. They care for sick and injured people, and their work often saves lives.

There are thought to be between **10–15 million doctors in the world.**

That's a lot, but we need another **4.3 million doctors** to help properly **care for** all the **people in the world.**

A **surgeon** is a specialist doctor who treats injuries and diseases by performing surgical operations.

STUDY TIME

It takes a long time to train to be a doctor, at least five or six years studying at college or university, then many more years of training at work after that.

When an emergency call is made, a **paramedic** is often the first person to arrive and help with an injury or problem.

A paramedic does three main things:

1. Figures out what the medical problems are.
2. Treats the problems at the place of the emergency.
3. Takes the injured person to hospital.

There are many **different types of doctors,** including:

1. An **obstetrician** (looks after women who are pregnant)

2. A **neurologist** (takes care of people with brain, spine, and nerve problems)

3. An **oncologist** (deals with cancer)

4. A **dermatologist** (helps solve skin problems)

5. A **cardiologist** (has special skills for treating heart conditions)

CHECK THIS OUT

A **primary care physician** (general practitioner) can use simple methods to check on someone's general health.

A doctor can check your blood pressure using a strap that goes around your arm.

If the pressure numbers are **too low or high,** there could be a problem with **how blood is pumped** around your body.

A **stethoscope** is used to listen to the sounds of the **heart** and **lungs.** A doctor knows how a healthy heart and lungs should sound.

A doctor uses an **otoscope** to shine light into the ear to check for **problems** or **infections.**

An **X-ray machine** lets a doctor see inside the body by making an **X-ray image.**

X-rays help a doctor see things like **broken bones, heart problems, some cancers,** and **curves in the spine.**

117

ARTIFICIAL INTELLIGENCE

Specialists have the technology to do amazing things to help a person who has a missing limb. Living a normal life is possible thanks to these ingenious solutions.

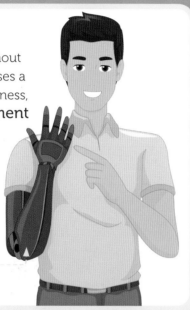

If a person is born without a part of the body or loses a part through injury or illness, an **artificial replacement** could be used.

An artificial body part, also called a **prosthesis**, could be a **hand, arm, leg**, or **foot**.

A medical worker who creates **artificial limbs** is a **prosthetist**.

There are three main parts of a **prosthetic limb:**

1. The **socket** is the part that **connects to the person's body.**

2. The **suspension system** keeps the prosthesis **attached to the body.** This can be a **strap** or **belt,** or it can use **suction** to stay on.

3 The **pylon** is the inside frame of the prosthesis. It can be made from **carbon, plastic,** or metal.

Modern prostheses are lightweight and highly technical, but simple artificial body parts were made hundreds of years ago.

An **artificial toe using wood** and **leather** was found in Egypt with the remains of a body.

The toe was nearly 3,000 years old!

A **special curved prosthetic leg,** often called a **blade,** can help an **athlete with a missing leg run very fast.**

Sprinters using a blade prosthetic leg can run the **100 m race in around 10.8 seconds.**

This is only 1.2 seconds slower than the fastest times by runners without artificial legs.

There are **amazing prosthetic arms** and **hands** that can grip and pick things up. They are often called **bionic arms.**

For this technology to work, a surgeon **reconnects muscle nerves** that would go to the missing limb to another part of the body, like the chest.

These new nerves still give off **an electrical signal,** and the bionic hand receives the signal and moves.

STRANGE STUFF

You'll be amazed at the facts behind some of the strange things our bodies do. Most happen for a reason and help to keep our bodies working properly.

SUPER SNEEZES

A sneeze is your body trying to get rid of something irritating the inside of the nose.

Nerves in the nose send a message to the brain, and the **body gets ready to sneeze.**

Muscles all around the body, such as in the **stomach, chest,** and **throat,** help you sneeze.

The eyelid muscles are also connected to sneezing—**the eyes always close during a sneeze!**

Hiccuping happens when the **diaphragm muscle,** at the bottom of the chest, is irritated.

The diaphragm is pulled down, and air **suddenly sucks into the throat.**

100

A sneeze cloud of spit and gas can leave the mouth at 160 kp/h (100 mph). That's much faster than cars are usually allowed to drive!

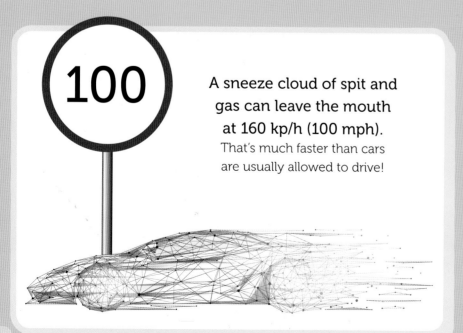

The vocal cords close quickly, and a hiccup sound comes out of your mouth!

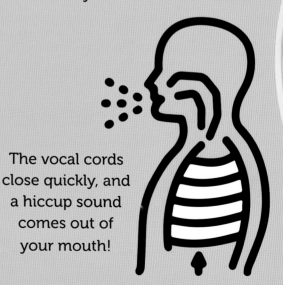

Scientists don't know for sure why humans yawn, but **there are two possible reasons:**

1. To bring more oxygen into the blood when we are bored or tired. When we are bored, we don't breathe as deeply.

2. To make the body feel awake by stretching the lungs and increasing the heart rate.

Medical professionals are also not sure why we dream. One reason could be that it **helps the brain process our thoughts, emotions, and experiences.**

Dreams could happen because of **chemical changes** and **electrical charges** that take place in the brain when we sleep.

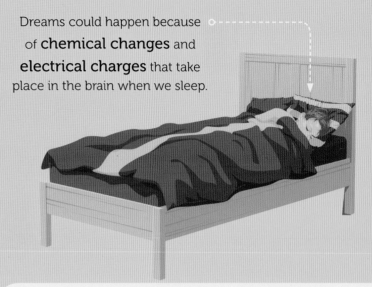

In an average lifetime, a person yawns **240,000 times!** Yawns usually last for about 6 seconds.

The **appendix** is a small organ attached to the large intestine. Its function is unknown. Some doctors think its job is to put **helpful bacteria into the digestive system.**

When a person chops an onion, their eyes may water—the **tears keep chemicals from the onion from irritating the eye.**

Tears come from **glands in the eyelid** and usually drain away from the **tear duct** in the corner of each eye, near the nose.

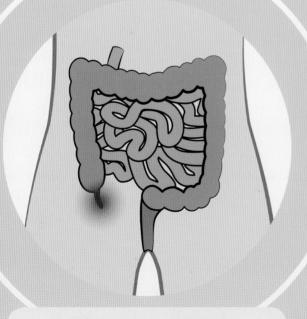

Our cheeks can look **red** when we are **embarrassed.**

Feeling **embarrassed releases a hormone** (chemical) called **adrenaline,** which makes blood vessels in the face get bigger so the cheeks look redder.

The **appendix** can become sore and painful. A surgeon will then take it out, and the body does not miss it at all!

IN THE FUTURE

Medicine and science have changed so much over the last 100 years and they are advancing all the time. Many more new developments will improve and change human healthcare over the next 100 years, and beyond.

Gene therapy is a technology where genes are used to **treat** or **prevent a disease**. Genes are the body's list of instructions inside every cell.

In the future, **gene therapy medicine** could be used to:

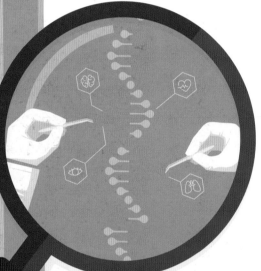

1. Replace a **mutated (faulty) gene** that causes disease with a healthy gene of the same type.

2. Put a new gene into the body to **cure an illness.**

3. Get rid of a **faulty gene that's not working.**

Robotic arms and **equipment** that can do operations are already being used and developed.

A robot arm controlled by a surgeon, is much **steadier and quicker than a human's.**

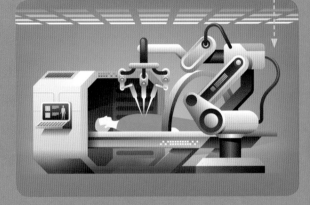

This could mean that **no mistakes** are made in surgery.

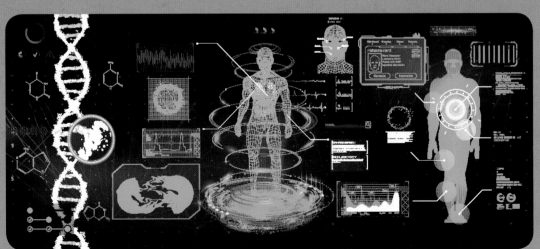

A system in the future using an **augmented reality (AR) headset** could let doctors see **organs inside a person's body.**

It could help find and cure problems **very quickly.**

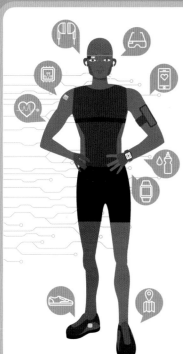

If people could **wear a sensor that detected problems with their body and health**, doctors could receive a message to take medical action if necessary.

This type of future medical system is known as **wearable technology.**

Digital contact lenses worn in the eye could help people with **diabetes..**

Sensors in the lens collect information from tears and detect when a **body's blood sugar levels change.**

Medical chatbots will be used a lot more in the future. A **chatbot** is an **automatic computer system that helps people work out what is wrong with them** before they talk to a doctor or nurse.

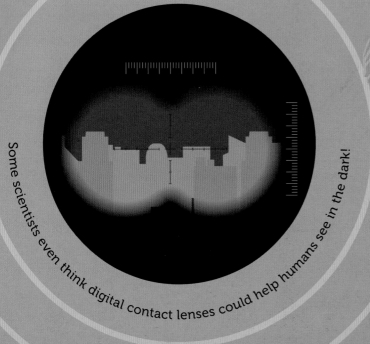

Some scientists even think digital contact lenses could help humans see in the dark!

In the future, **robotic exoskeleton suits** will hopefully help people with severe injuries to **walk again.**

The clever technology **helps move legs, knees, and hips.** These suits could be expensive, though, costing about $40,000 (£32,000).

FAMOUS DISCOVERIES AND PEOPLE

We know so much about the body and how to look after it, thanks to all the hard work and discoveries made around the world by doctors and scientists throughout history.

Early 1500s

Over 500 years ago, Italian artist and scientist **Leonardo da Vinci** sketched and made important notes about how the body worked. This is called **anatomy**.

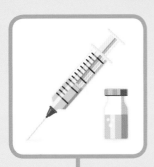

1849

Elizabeth Blackwell became the **first female doctor** in the United States. In 1857, she helped set up the **New York Infirmary for Women and Children**.

1796

Edward Jenner's experiment on a 12 year old in England successfully made a **vaccine** against the disease **smallpox**.

1628

William Harvey, an English doctor, published a book explaining, for the first time that the **heart pumped blood around the body**.

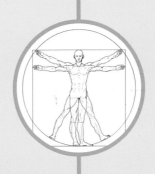

1861

The French scientist **Louis Pasteur** discovered that **germs caused illness**. His work led to better knowledge of diseases like **cholera** and **anthrax**.

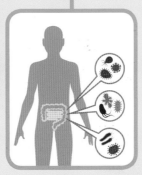

1816

The **stethoscope** was invented in France by **René Laennec**. It enables a **doctor** to listen to a person's heartbeat.

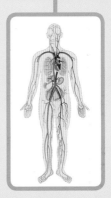

1941
Howard Florey, an Australian, and **Ernst Chain**, from Germany, developed **penicillin** even further. Their work meant that it could be given to **soldiers during World War II**.

1967
Christiaan Barnard, from South Africa, performed the first heart transplant. A heart transplant is when a **heart from a dead person is placed inside a living person**.

1881
After hearing about the international aid work of Swiss humanitarian **Henry Dunant's Red Cross,** American, **Clara Barton** went to Europe to serve as a Red Cross nurse in the **Franco-Prussian war**. This inspired her to set up the **American Red Cross.**

1895
A clever German physicist named **William Roentgen** discovered **X-rays**, which enabled doctors to **see bones** and **organs inside the body.**

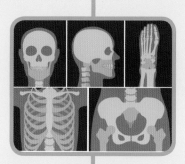

1951
English scientist **Rosalind Franklin** did lots of work in the early 1950s that was essential in helping us to understand **DNA**.

1928
The famous Scottish doctor, **Alexander Fleming,** was the first person to discover penicillin, which could be used to treat some common illnesses.

1962
Ronald Malt and his team of surgeons in Massachusetts, united States, **reattached the arm of a boy** after he had an accident. It was the first time a limb had been reconnected.

1893
African-American **Daniel Hale Williams**, saved the life of a man with stab wounds by **operating on his heart**. This is thought to be the first successful heart operation.

1949
Canadian surgeons **Wilfred Bigalow** and **John Callaghan** revealed that **hypothermia** (lowering the body's temperature) allowed for **better heart surgery**. They also worked on the **heart pacemaker.**

1941
Howard Florey, an Australian, and **Ernst Chain**, from Germany, developed **penicillin** even further. Their work meant that it could be given to **soldiers during World War II.**

1967
Christiaan Barnard, from South Africa, performed the first heart transplant. A heart transplant is when a **heart from a dead person is placed inside a living person.**

1895
A clever German physicist named **William Roentgen** discovered **X-rays**, which enabled doctors to **see bones** and **organs inside the body.**

1881
After hearing about the international aid work of Swiss humanitarian **Henry Dunant's Red Cross**, American, **Clara Barton** went to Europe to serve as a Red Cross nurse in the **Franco-Prussian war.** This inspired her to set up the **American Red Cross.**

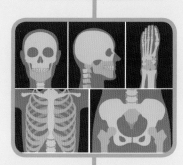

1951
English scientist **Rosalind Franklin** did lots of work in the early 1950s that was essential in helping us to understand **DNA.**

1928
The famous Scottish doctor, **Alexander Fleming**, was the first person to discover penicillin, which could be used to treat some common illnesses.

1962
Ronald Malt and his team of surgeons in Massachusetts, united States, **reattached the arm of a boy** after he had an accident. It was the first time a limb had been reconnected.

1893
African-American **Daniel Hale Williams**, saved the life of a man with stab wounds by **operating on his heart.** This is thought to be the first successful heart operation.

1949
Canadian surgeons **Wilfred Bigalow** and **John Callaghan** revealed that **hypothermia** (lowering the body's temperature) allowed for **better heart surgery.** They also worked on the **heart pacemaker.**

GLOSSARY

ANTIBODY
Known as immunoglobulin, antibodies in blood detect harmful invaders such as bacteria and viruses and eliminate them.

ARTERY
A blood vessel that carries blood from the heart toward the tissues.

ATOM
The smallest unit of an element.

BACTERIA
A living thing made of a single cell and is a type of germ that can enter and live in the body.

CARBOHYDRATE
One of a group of substances, which includes glucose, starch, and cellulose, that can be broken down to release energy in the body.

CARTILAGE
The springy substance that cushions bone ends in joints, and provides flexibility and support.

CELL
Each living thing is made of structures called cells. Humans have 30 to 40 trillion cells.

CHROMOSOME
A collection of genes made up of DNA. Humans have 46 chromosomes in each cell.

COLLAGEN
A tough, fibrous protein that gives strength to tendons and other tissues.

DNA
Deoxyribonucleic acid, or DNA, is a structure with a double helix shape that forms genes and is found in a cell's nucleus.

ELEMENT
A pure substance made from one type of atom.

ENZYME
A protein that speeds up a chemical reaction.

GENE
A unit of DNA that develops a person's characteristics, and which is usually located on a chromosome.

GERMS
Microscopic organisms that can invade a body and may release toxins (harmful substances) to make a person feel unwell. Not all germs are harmful.

GLAND
Any organ that lets out a chemical to do a particular task.